LOST LONDON

LOST
LONDON

Richard Guard

Michael O'Mara Books Limited

For Kirsty, Oliver, Isaac and Alfred
Seized by a compulsion you long to discover Drayton Park.
Go there at once and miss a turn. *The London Game*, Seven Towns Ltd, 1972

First published in Great Britain in 2012 by
Michael O'Mara Books Limited
9 Lion Yard
Tremadoc Road
London sw4 7NQ

A CIP catalogue record for this book is available from the British Library.

Papers used by Michael O'Mara Books Limited are natural, recyclable
products made from wood grown in sustainable forests. The manufacturing
processes conform to the environmental regulations of the country of origin.

ISBN: 978-1843178033 in paperback print format
ISBN: 978-1-84317-896-5 in EPub format
ISBN: 978-1-84317-895-8 in Mobipocket format

1 2 3 4 5 6 7 8 9 10

Printed and bound in Great Britain by Clays Ltd, St Ives plc

Designed and typeset by Design 23

Picture research by Judith Palmer.
Jacket picture sources: *Antiquities of London and Its Environs, Antiquities of
Westminster*, both by John Thomas Smith; *Father Thames* by Walter Higgins;
London by Walter Besant; Knight's London, Vols. I, V, VI; *The Mirror of
Literature, Amusement, and Instruction*, Vols. XII & XIX; *Old and New
London*, Vols. I, II, VI, by Walter Thornbury and Edward Walford; *The Old
Bailey and Newgate* by Charles Gordon; *A Short History of the English People*,
Vol. II, by J. R. Green. Page 24 www.clipart.com

www.mombooks.com

Contents

INTRODUCTION   9

Ackerman's *The Strand*   11

Adam and Eve Tea Gardens *Tottenham Court Road*   12

Agar Town *Kings Cross*   13

Alhambra *Leicester Square*   14

Alsatia *Temple*   15

Archery   17

Astley's *Westminster Bridge Road*   18

Atmospheric Railway *Southwark*   20

Barbican *EC2*   21

Bartholomew Fair *Smithfield*   22

Baynard's Castle *Blackfriars*   25

Bedlam, or St Bethlehem's Hospital *Liverpool Street*   27

Bishopsgate   29

Bon Marché *Brixton*   29

Bridewell *Banks of River Fleet*   30

Carlisle House *Soho Square*   32

Charing Cross   33

Chelsea Bun House   34

Chippendale's Workshop *Covent Garden*   35

Clare Market *Aldwych*   36

Coldbath Fields Prison *Clerkenwell*   38

Colosseum *Regent's Park*   40

Costermongers' Language   41

Crapper and Company Ltd *Chelsea*   42

Cremorne Gardens *Chelsea*   42

Crossing Sweepers   44

The Devil Public House *Fleet Street*   46

Dioramas   47

The Dog and Duck *Southwark*   48

Dog Finders   49
Don Saltero's Coffee House *Chelsea*   50
Durham House *The Strand*   52
Eel Pie House *Highbury*   54
Effra River, *South London*   55
Egyptian Hall *Piccadilly*   56
Enon Chapel *Near the Strand*   58
Essex House *Near the Strand*   60
Euston Arch   62
Execution Dock *Wapping*   63
Exeter House *The Strand*   64
Farringdon Market   66
Fauconberg House *Soho*   68
Field of the Forty Footsteps *Russell Square*   69
Fleet Marriages   70
Fleet Prison *Blackfriars*   72
Fleet River   73
Frost Fairs   75
Gaiety Theatre *The Strand*   77
Gamages *High Holburn*   79
Gentleman's Magazine   80
The Globe *Bankside*   81
Goodman's Fields Theatre *Whitechapel*   83
Gore House *Kensington*   85
The Great Globe *Leicester Square*   86
Gunter's Tea Shop *Mayfair*   87
Hanover Square Rooms   89
Harringay Stadium   90
Highbury Barn   91
Hippodrome Racecourse *Ladbroke Grove*   93
Hockley-in-the-Hole *Clerkenwell*   94
Holborn Restaurant   96

Holy Trinity *Minories Tower Hill*	97
Horn Fair *Charlton*	98
Islington Spa, Or The New Tunbridge Wells	100
Jacob's Island *Bermondsey*	102
Jenny's Whim *Pimlico*	104
Jonathan's Coffee House *Bank*	105
Kilburn Wells	106
King's Bench Prison *Borough*	107
King's Wardrobe *Blackfriars*	109
Kingsway Theatre *Holborn*	110
Leicester House *Soho*	111
Lillie Bridge Grounds *Earls Court*	112
Lincoln's Inn Fields Theatre	113
London Bridge *Some Notable Decapitated Heads*	
Displayed Thereon	115
London Bridge Waterworks	116
London Salvage Corps	117
Lowther Arcade *The Strand*	118
Lyons Corner Houses	120
Molly Houses	121
Mudlarks	122
Necropolis Railway *Waterloo*	123
Newgate Prison *Old Bailey*	125
New River Head *Clerkenwell*	128
Nine Elms Railway Station	129
Nonsuch House *London Bridge*	130
Old Clothes Exchange *Houndsditch*	131
Old Slaughter's Coffee House *Covent Garden*	132
Pantheon *Oxford Street*	133
Paris Gardens *Bankside*	135
Patterers, or Death Hunters	137
Penny Gaffs	138

Peerless Pool *Shoreditch*   140
Pillory   141
Plague Pits   142
Pure Collectors   144
Queen's Hall *Langham Place*   145
Rainbow Coffee House *Fleet Street*   147
Ranelagh Gardens *Chelsea*   147
Ratcliffe Highway *Wapping*   150
Rillington Place *Ladbroke Grove*   152
Rivers   155
The Rookeries   156
Rosemary Lane *Tower Hill*   158
St George's Fields *Southwark*   160
St Paul's Cathedral   161
Salmon's Waxworks *Covent Garden*   164
Silvertown Explosives Factory *West Ham*   165
Slang   166
Steelyard *Canon Street*   171
Street Cries   172
Street Traders   174
Tabard Inn *Borough*   177
Thorney Island *Westminster*   178
Toshers   180
Tyburn *Marble Arch*   181
Vauxhall Gardens *Lambeth*   183
Walbrook   186
Watermen   187
Whitehall Palace *Westminster*   188
Wren's Lost Churches   189
INDEX   190

INTRODUCTION

London is a very old and magnificent city – but its buildings are not that ancient. Although it has been inhabited for 2000 years few traces are left from that time. Tiny sections of the old wall and the London Stone from which the Romans measured distances throughout the land, are all that remain. Mosaics, foundations and artefacts have been frequently uncovered, but there's no colosseum, amphitheatre or Parthenon to mark 400 years of Roman rule.

The medieval period too has little to show for itself – a few churches claim to have been established in the 10th century, but the oldest existing building is William the Conqueror's White Tower, the original Tower of London, built in 1085.

A series of rapid expansions and terrible disasters have stripped the capital of its age old monuments. Most famous is the Great Fire of 1666 which destroyed 90 per cent of the old city. Over ten thousand new dwellings were built in its aftermath – none are left – the German Blitz destroyed the last of these.

Much of the city built between the Great Fire and the death of Queen Victoria in 1901 – the city immortalized in the works of Charles Dickens – was swept away with modernizing and moralizing zeal. Massive urban development consumed the fields where city dwellers once took their pleasures. The railways sliced through ancient thoroughfares and demolished districts that had stood for hundreds of years. Many fabulous and remarkable buildings were simply removed because they were old.

Now only a few glorious pockets of 18th century London remain. It would be a fool's errand to attempt to describe all that has been lost – indeed it would be impossible. This humble book only aims to amuse its readers by describing some of the buildings and streets, the jobs and habits, the markets, fairs and pastimes that have made London what it is today, the greatest city in the world.

London has been the epicentre of so many important historical events – in politics, in the arts, in science – that for lovers of the capital the very streets seem to reverberate with echo of voices past. In compiling this book I have attempted, where possible, to find a contemporaneous quote that brings the location and the time and place back to life, so that the reader will be able to walk the city's streets and people them with the great rush of humanity that have called London their home for the last 2000 years.

RG, East Dulwich, 2012

Ackerman's

The Strand

OPENED BY RUDOLPH ACKERMAN, AN
Anglo-German bookseller and print-maker, this
shop was not only the first art library in England
but also the first to be lit by gas 'which burns with
a purity and brilliance unattainable by any other
mode of illumination'.

The building had been an art school from 1750 until
1806, attended by such notable figures as William Blake,
Richard Cosway and Francis Wheatley. Beginning in 1813,
Ackerman held soirées each Wednesday attended by the great
and good, many of whom were attracted by the fact that he was
a prominent employer of aristocrats and priests who had fled
the French Revolution. As well as selling books, prints, fancy
goods and artists' materials, it was for many years the 'meeting
place of the best social life in London'.

Ackerman was also a notable publisher. Each month from
1809 to 1828, he printed *The Repository of Arts, Literature,
Commerce and Manufactures*, a major historical source of
information on Regency fashion and a treasure trove for
modern makers of Jane Austen period dramas. Meanwhile, his
The Microcosm of London, or London in Miniature (1808–1810)
contains hand-coloured aquatints of many since-lost city views.
Ackerman's publishing business ended in 1858 and the site of
his shop is now home to the legendary restaurant, Simpson's-
in-the-Strand.

Adam and Eve Tea Gardens

Tottenham Court Road

FROM 1628 UNTIL THE LATE 1700S, CITY DWELLERS
tired of the hustle and bustle of life could take a
stroll to this countryside tea garden famous for its
tea and cake.

Located on what is today one of London's most filthy
traffic junctions where the Euston, Tottenham Court and
Hampstead Roads meet, this public house was known for
its quiet orchards of wild fruit trees.

Its reputation declined as building developments
encroached, with Larwood reporting the arrival of
'highwaymen, footpads, pickpockets, and low women'.
By the early 19th century the gardens were surrounded by
houses notorious as hang-outs for prostitutes and criminals.
The public house was subsequently closed by magistrates
although it reopened as a tavern for a short time in 1813.

Agar Town

King's Cross

**CHARLES DICKENS DESCRIBED THE SLUM
that grew up here from 1840 as 'a suburban
Connemara … wretched hovels, the doors
blocked up with mud, heaps of ash, oyster shells
and decayed vegetables, the stench on a rainy
morning is enough to knock down a bullock'.**

The 72-acre site was previously the property of William Agar, a notorious litigant whose complaints even forced a change of direction in the intended route of the Regent's Canal.

After Agar's death in 1838, the shanty town in King's Cross emerged when his widow sub-let the land. In 1851 one W M Thomas, a visitor to London, described his journey through the area: 'The footpath, gradually narrowing, merged at length in the bog of the road. I hesitated; but to turn back was almost as dangerous as to go on. I thought, too, of the possibility of my wandering through the labyrinth of rows and crescents until I should be benighted; and the idea of a night in Agar Town, without a single lamp to guide my footsteps, emboldened me to proceed. Plunging at once into the mud, and hopping in the manner of a kangaroo – so as not to allow myself time to sink and disappear altogether – I found myself, at length, once more in the King's Road.'

Among the slum's most famous residents was the boxer Tom Sawyer, while the music hall star Dan Leno was born here in December 1860. The Midlands Railway Company bought Agar Town in 1866 and demolished it to make way for the railways. Such was the area's poor reputation that there was little protest, even though its residents received no compensation. Today its name lives on in Agar Grove, a street running along the old slum's northern boundary.

Alhambra

Leicester Square

Built in a broadly Moorish style with two minarets, the Alhambra had a variety of different names and purposes. Originally opened in 1854 as the Royal Panopticon of Arts and Science, it boasted a huge hall, hydraulic lift, lecture theatre and 97ft-high fountain.

This initial venture was a failure and in 1856 its exhibits, displaying scientific wonders of the age, were sold off for a mere £8,000 – 10 per cent of what it cost to build.

Two years later the building reopened as a circus and from 1861 served as a music hall. Featured performers included Charles Blondin, who had recently tightrope-walked across Niagara Falls, and Jules Léotard, whose performances inspired the song 'The Daring Young Man on the Flying Trapeze' (and after whom the tight-fitting one-piece garment is named). However, the Alhambra lost its entertainment licence in 1870 after hosting the first London performance of the Can-Can, during which the dancer 'Wiry Sal' lifted her foot 'higher than her head several times towards the audience and had been much applauded'.

For the next decade it staged plays and promenade concerts before burning down in 1883. The following year it returned as a music hall and became a venue for ballet in 1919. The theatre was demolished in 1936 and where it once stood, facing into Leicester Square, is now an Odeon cinema. The Alhambra name does live on in Alhambra House on nearby Charing Cross Road, though rather than a palace of entertainment it is a somewhat miserable black marble-fronted building housing offices and a bank.

Alsatia

Temple

THE NAME ALSATIA DERIVES FROM THE LONG-disputed Alsace region on the French–German border that was historically outside normal legislative jurisdiction.

In London, Alsatia covers the area formerly occupied by London's Whitefriars monastery, which is commemorated in an eponymous street that runs south from Fleet Street towards the River Thames.

After he dissolved the religious orders, Henry VIII

parcelled out monastic lands to his favourites and so Alsatia was given to his physician, Doctor Butts. The area soon deteriorated into a maze of alleyways and squalid housing. Yet the idea of medieval religious sanctuary lived on in the area and from the 15th until the 17th century, the population defended itself against any bailiff or city official who tried to enter the area to arrest any of its inhabitants. However, by Elizabeth 1's time attempts were being made to clean up the area, as the State Papers record:

'Item. These gates shalbe orderly shutt and opened at convenient times, and porters appointed for the same. Also, a scavenger to keep the precincte clean.

Item. Tipling houses shalbe bound for good order.

Item. Searches to be made by the constables, with the assistance of the inhabitants, at the commandmente of the justices.

Item. The poore within the precincte shalbe provyded for by the inhabitantes of the same.

Item. In tyme of plague, good order shalbe taken for the restrainte of the same.

Item. Lanterne and light to be mainteined duringe winter time.'

But these attempts had little or no effect and, surprisingly, the area's liberties where enshrined in 1608 when James 1 granted it a charter.

It was once said of Alsatia that 'the dregs of the age that was indeed full of dregs, vatted in that disreputable sanctuary east of the Temple'. It was immortalised in two major literary works, Thomas Shadwell's *The Squire of Alsatia* and Sir Walter Scott's *The Fortunes of Nigel*, both of which drew vivid pictures of this ramshackle kingdom where people defended their liberties at all costs. Shadwell, for instance, depicted the following scene:

'An arrest! An arrest!' and in a moment they are 'up in the Friars,' with a cry of 'fall on.' The skulking debtors scuttle into their burrows, the bullies fling down cup and can, lug out their rusty blades, and rush into the mêlée. From every den and crib red-faced, bloated women hurry with fire-forks, spits, cudgels, pokers, and shovels. They're 'up in the Friars,' with a vengeance!

In 1678 an Act of Parliament abolished the liberties of Alsatia and several other areas in the city, including The Minories, Salisbury Court, Mitre Court, Baldwins Gardens and Stepney. In 1723 London's last two sanctuaries – at The Mint in Southwark and The Savoy – were finally abolished. However, the spirit of lawless autonomy lived on in many of these areas for years to come and grew elsewhere, as in the notorious 'Rookeries' that survived until the late Victorian era.

Archery

IN 1369 AN ACT OF PARLIAMENT DECREED
that Londoners must practise archery and 'that
everyone of the said city of London strong of
body, at leisure times and on holidays, use in their
recreations bows and arrows'.

Despite the decline of the longbow as a potent military weapon over the preceeding 300 years, both Henry VIII and Elizabeth I tried to re-establish the practice. In 1627 archery regiments were formed by the City of London and practised annually in Finsbury, St George's Fields and Moorfields. But towards the end of the 18th century urban encroachment forced the archers further away, with the Royal Toxophilite Society (founded 1781) eventually being driven to move from its Regent's Park home to Buckinghamshire. Several parts of London maintain an association with the activity, such as the Archery Tavern, Bayswater, and Newington Butts at the Elephant and Castle.

Astley's

Westminster Bridge Road

ORIGINALLY CALLED ROYAL GROVE, ASTLEY'S WAS London's first circus. It was opened by a former cavalry officer, Philip Astley, who received a licence for his enterprise after he used his Herculean proportions to help George III subdue a runaway horse.

When his original site burned down in 1794, he rebuilt it as Astley's Amphitheatre. Shows often featured clowns, acrobats and conjurers, and there were vast spectaculars featuring, for instance, 'several hundred performers and fifty-two horses, two lions, kangaroos, pelicans, reindeer and a chamois'. Other entertainments included sword fights and exotic melodramas. The venue, though, was plagued by fires and had to be rebuilt in 1803, 1841 and 1862, when it reopened as the New Westminster Theatre.

It was finally demolished in 1893. Charles Dickens was an avid Astley's fan as both a child and adult, writing of it fondly in *Sketches by Boz*.

Atmospheric Railway

South East London

1845 SAW THE OPENING OF A REMARKABLE and revolutionary form of railway transport, powered not by steam but by compressed air.

Designed in Southwark by Samuel Clegg and the Samuda brothers, a line ran from Forest Hill to West Croydon with carriages driven by a piston connected to a pipe running between the rails.

A pumping station at either end of the track provided the air. With the trains unable to pass over the tracks of the regular railway at Norwood, Clegg and the Samudas built the world's first railway flyover, which is still in use today.

The system was plagued by technical difficulties, mainly due to metal corrosion and wear and tear on leather seals. Indeed, passengers were frequently forced to push trains between stations when the pressure failed. Another major problem stemmed from the quietness of the trains, which somewhat perversely unnerved passengers.

By 1846 the cost of breakdowns and repairs forced the London and Croydon Railway Company to abandon its experiment and turn to the more reliable power of steam. But this wasn't the end of atmospheric and pneumatic transport in London. In 1863 the Post Office built two tunnels out of Euston Station, one running half a mile to a sorting office and the other to St Paul's in the City. Using pneumatic trains, the journey to St Paul's took a mere nine minutes. The route ran until 1874 but high costs forced its closure. When the Tube system was first conceived, pneumatic power was again considered, and construction of such a line between Whitehall and Waterloo even got under way until a financial crisis in 1866 halted work that was never restarted.

Barbican

EC2

Named after the outer fortifications
of the city, the original Barbican was most likely a
watch-tower, which the great historian of London,
John Stow, said was pulled down in the reign of Henry
III. In the 16th and 17th centuries the area became well
known for its market in new and used clothes.

Much of the locality was destroyed in the Great Fire of 1666 and was again devastated in the Blitz during the Second World War, when thirty-two acres were completely razed. Six major historic streets and numerous other courts and alley-ways were lost forever in the bombing. Amongst them were Jewin Cresent and Jewin Street, which had been the site of a Jewish enclave and burial ground until the expulsion of the Jews from England in 1290.

John Milton was a resident here when he wrote *Paradise Lost*, while Redcross Street was formerly the home of the Abbot of Ramsey (as well as the site of a red cross that was still standing in the 16th century during Stow's lifetime). Other places of interest included Paper Street, replete with warehouses for paper, and Silver Street, a hub for the city's silversmiths. Elsewhere, Australia Avenue, built relatively recently in 1894 between Barbican and Jewin Crescent, was much used by those active in Antipodean trade. However, such was the destruction wrought between 1939 and 1945 that it was decided to rebuild the entire area on a new plan, creating the Barbican Centre that we have today, the largest multi-arts venue in Europe.

Bartholomew Fair

Smithfield

**OF ALL THE GREAT CITY FAIRS,
Bartholomew Fair was the oldest and most famous.
It was held at West Smithfield, the site of modern-
day Smithfield Market.**

It was first celebrated in 1133 when Rahere, the founder of the local priory, was granted a charter to raise money for a new hospital, the now famous St Bartholomew. For the next 400 years Bartholomew was the primary cloth fair in the country, held over three days from each 24th August, the feast day of St Bartholomew. It was traditionally opened by the Lord Mayor, who would ride from the Guildhall to Smithfield to read the opening proclamation at the Fair's entrance – having stopped on his way for a jug of wine spiced with nutmeg and sugar supplied by the keeper of Newgate. In 1688, one unfortunate Mayor, Sir John Shorter, closed his tankard lid with such violence that his horse bolted, dismounting the venerable gent, who died of his injuries the next day.

The mood of the event began to change at the beginning of the 17th century, when the city's cloth dealers began to explore national and international markets outside of London. The fair evolved instead into an opportunity for general merriment and over the next century became increasingly rowdy, now less a trade fair than a joyous celebration and public holiday, complete with plays, puppet shows, freak shows and exotic animals. Samuel Pepys wrote of the experience in his diary:

Thence away by coach to Bartholomew Fayre, with my wife, and showed her the monkeys dancing on the ropes, which was strange, but such dirty sport that I was not pleased with it. There was also a horse with hoofs like rams hornes, a goose with four feet, and a cock with three. Thence to another place, and we saw a poor fellow, whose legs were tied behind his back, dance upon his hands with his arse above his head, and also dance upon his crutches, without any legs upon the ground to help him, which he did with that pain that I was sorry to see it, and did pity him and give him money after he had done.

The year 1817 witnessed the appearance of Toby, a 'real

learned pig' who, with twenty handkerchiefs covering his eyes, could tell the time to the minute and pick out cards from a pack. Meanwhile, Thomas Horne recorded seeing 'four lively little crocodiles hatched from eggs at Peckham by steam'. But the drunken debauchery among visitors to the fair began to irk the city authorities. In 1801, for instance, a gang of thieves surrounded a respectable lady and tore the clothes from her back, while a year later random victims were attacked with cudgels and several windows were broken.

In 1815 alone the Guildhall heard forty-five cases of felony, misdemeanor and assault committed at Bartholomew and so the city embarked on a concerted effort to clean up the event. Many of the raucous shows and booths were moved to Islington and by 1840 only the animal shows still remained. By 1849 the fair amounted to little more than a few gingerbread stalls and in 1850, Lord Mayor Musgrove turned up for the opening ceremony to find no one there. Five years later even this 700-year-old ceremony was abandoned and London's greatest fair was consigned to history.

Baynard's Castle

Blackfriars

THE NAME REFERS TO TWO CASTLES THAT WERE in roughly the same area, east of the current Blackfriars Bridge. The first was a Norman-built castle demolished by King John in 1213 after he was jilted by its owner's daughter.

Legend tells that the King took a fancy to Matilda Fitzwater (known as 'the Fair'), daughter of the master of the house, but she would not consent to become his mistress. Her father fled and she was carried off to the Tower of London, only to be poisoned with powder sprinkled on to her poached egg.

The second castle was built fifty years later and about a

hundred yards east of the original. (Some other land from the Fitzwater estate was gifted to the Dominican order of monks, giving rise to the area becoming known as Blackfriars). The new fortress eventually became a royal household, with Edward IV crowned there in 1452, followed by both Lady Jane Grey and Mary I in 1553. During the reign of Henry VIII it served as the home to three of his wives – Katherine of Aragon, Anne Boleyn and Anne of Cleves.

Pepys wrote that Charles II stayed here in 1660 but the building, reportedly 'one of the most interesting in London', was destroyed in the Great Fire of 1666 and never rebuilt, although one tower remained until 1720. Excavation of the site in the 1970s revealed that much of the castle's outer limits were built upon the remains of a Roman wall that ran along the river bank, the existence of which had been disputed for many years.

Bedlam, or St Bethlehem's Hospital

Liverpool Street

THERE HAVE BEEN THREE SEPARATE SITES FOR this most famous of mental hospitals. The first was at Bishopsgate, on the site of modern-day Liverpool Street railway station. Established in 1329 as a regular hospital run by the Priory of St Mary Bethlehem, by 1377 it was taking in 'distracted' patients.

Treatment was unsophisticated and often cruel, with inmates commonly chained, beaten, whipped and ducked.

With the dissolution of the monasteries under Henry VIII, 'Bedlam' fell under the control of Bridewell, a local prison. The already deplorable conditions for inmates continued to deteriorate. Eventually a grand new building was opened at Moorfields around 1675–76, designed by Robert Hook and with a front entrance adorned by two famous sculptures of *Madness* and *Melancholy* by Caius Cibber. These figures are all that remains of the second Bedlam and now reside in the Victoria & Albert Museum. A version of them can also be seen in the chilling final plate of Hogarth's *The Rake's Progress*.

Much of the Hospital's income was derived from admitting visitors to view the 'idiots'. It became a popular holiday destination for many city dwellers over the next 100

years, until the practise was outlawed in 1770 as it 'tended to disturb the equilibrium of the patients'. From then on, visitor numbers were controlled and sightseers had to buy a ticket in advance to get in.

By 1800, Hook's great building, once described as a match for the Tuileries Palace in Paris, was starting to decay, with the blame laid on cheap materials. So a new site for the hospital was found in St George's Fields, Southwark (above). Patients were moved there in 1815 and conditions gradually improved. In 1851 a resident doctor was appointed, although the habit of viewing inmates remained ever popular. A balcony at the Grand Union pub on Brook Street was specially built to overlook the gardens and is still there to this day. The last patients left the institution in 1930 and the building was reopened in 1936 as the Imperial War Museum.

Bishopgate

**ONE OF THE EIGHT ORIGINAL GATES TO THE city,
standing at Bishopsgate and Camomile Street.**

The others included Aldgate, Moorgate, Cripplegate, Aldersgate, Newgate and Ludgate – all of which were demolished to increase the flow of traffic in the period 1760–61. The only one that remains is Temple Bar.

Bon Marché

Brixton

**JAMES SMITH, A PRINTER FROM TOOTING, WON
a fortune at Newmarket races in 1877 and
proceeded to reinvent himself as Rosebery Smith.**

With his newfound riches he opened the city's first purpose-built department store. Why he chose 442–444 Brixton Road is anyone's guess, but the name he decided upon was Bon Marché, after the famous store in Paris. Unfortunately, Smith was no great businessman and he soon went bankrupt. The store, however, went on for almost another 100 years, declining only after the Second World War. It briefly became the Brixton Fair before closing for good in the 1970s.

Bridewell

Banks of River Fleet

A ROYAL PALACE BUILT BETWEEN 1515
and 1520 on the western bank of the Fleet River,
it was mainly used for entertaining visiting
foreign dignitaries, most notably the Holy Roman
Emperor, Charles v. On a visit in 1522, he
enjoyed tennis, feasts, music and pageants here.

Hans Holbein painted his famous *The Ambassadors* at the
palace and it was also the site of the Papal Legatine inquiry
into the marriage of Henry VIII and Katherine of Aragon.
Bridewell provided the backdrop for Katherine's famous and

noble speech in which she defended her position:

This 20 years or more I have been your true wife and by me ye have had divers children, although it hath pleased God to call them from this world, which hath been no default in me ... And when ye had me at first, I take God to my judge, I was a true maid, without touch of man. And whether this be true or no, I put it to your conscience ... Therefore, I humbly require you to spare me the extremity of this new court ... And if ye will not, to God I commit my cause.

Perhaps because of the unfortunate events played out here, Henry's son, Edward VI, gave up Bridewell Palace after being nagged to do so by Archbishop Ridley. In a sermon, Ridley had asked the King to provide a place for 'the strumpet and the idle person, the rioter... and the vagabond' and so Bridewell thenceforth became a house of correction for short-term prisoners. Floggings were held twice a week, and a ducking stool and stocks had been installed by 1638. Hogarth immortalized the place in plate 4 of *The Harlot's Progress*, which shows the harlot beating hemp as a punishment.

Bridewell also took in a number of orphans and destitute children, known for the blue uniforms they wore. It became both a school and a prison and in 1700 was the first jail to appoint its own medical staff. The model was so successful that the regime was copied and the name came to be used at other institutions in the city at Westminster and Clerkenwell, as well as further afield in Norwich and Edinburgh. The original Bridewell was eventually closed in 1855 and its location is today the site of Unilever House.

Carlisle House

Soho Square

BUILT IN 1685 FOR THE SECOND EARL
of Carlisle, this was a private home for many decades
before hosting an upholstery company and then
becoming the lodgings of the Neapolitan Ambassador.

In 1759 it was rented out to a Venetian society belle, Mrs Cornelys. A lady who scorned social mores, she converted the building into a venue for masquerades, card evenings and musical concerts, some of which were directed by the composer J S Bach. Increasingly risqué events led to the extravagant Mrs Cornelys being repeatedly fined for keeping a 'disorderly house'.

Although initially massively popular, the venue started to decline with the opening of the Pantheon on Oxford Street in 1772. Desperate to retain the house's reputation as the premier society venue, she undertook once again to refurbish it, even more grandiosely this time. The debts she incurred crippled her business and she was arrested and imprisoned in October 1772 at the King's Bench Prison, where she died in 1797. Amongst her various claims to fame was that Casanova was the father of her daughter.

For several years the rooms continued as a house of entertainment but garnered a much less salubrious clientele. One foreign visitor described the guests thus: 'The ladies were rigged in gaudy attire, attended by bucks, bloods and macaronis ...' The house closed in 1781 and was demolished in 1791, the site redeveloped as St Patrick's Catholic Church.

Charing Cross

ALSO KNOWN AS ELEANOR'S CROSS ERECTED BY Edward I, King of England (1272-1307) following the death of his wife of 46 years, Eleanor of Castille in 1290.

When she died, near Lincoln, her body was transported to Westminster, a journey that took twelve days. Edward had a memorial cross erected at every resting place of her funeral procession. The last at the village of Charing, a stopover between the City of London and Westminster.

Originally constructed of wood it was replaced by a cross of Caen stone, octagonal in shape, with smooth marble steps and decorated with eight statues. Removed by Parliamentary Act of 1643, it was not actually taken away until 1647, the stone reputedly being used to pave Whitehall.

The cross built in the forecourt of Charing Cross Station is a Victorian replacement, 180 yards away from its former location now marked by a statue of Charles I on horseback looking down Whitehall. For many years this spot was used to measure distances from London, replacing St Paul's, and prior to that the London Stone, the Roman mile-post in Cannon Street. London taxi drivers are required to know all the streets within a six-mile radius of Charing Cross, a principal that was instituted in 1865.

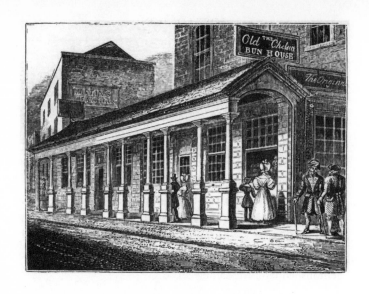

Chelsea Bun House

Pimlico

OPENING IN THE EARLY 1700S IN JEW'S ROW
(now Pimlico Road), this is where Chelsea buns
were invented. In its day, the Bun House was hugely
famous, prompting Jonathan Swift to celebrate the
'Rrrrrrrare Chelsea buns' after he visited in 1711.

Its proprietor, Richard Hand, decorated the interior with
clocks and a collection of curious artefacts. The Bun House
even found popularity among royalty, with both George II
and George III, their wives and children all visiting.

So successful was the business that on Good Fridays,

crowds of over 50,000 gathered outside the premises to purchase its products. The crush was such that in 1793 Mrs Hand issued a notice that 'respectfully informed her friends and customers that in consequence of the great concourse of people Good Friday last by which her neighbours have been much alarmed and annoyed … she is determined, though much to her loss, not to sell Cross Buns on that day'.

In 1804 the closure of the nearby Ranelagh Gardens had a profound effect on trade and the business began to decline. Yet even so, on Good Friday 1839 the House sold a staggering 240,000 buns. Nonetheless, the building was demolished later the same year.

Chippendale's Workshop

Covent Garden

In December 1753, the renowned cabinet-maker, Thomas Chippendale, leased the building at 60–61 St Martin's Lane in Covent Garden. It was from here that he published the legendary *Gentlemen and Cabinet Maker's Directory*.

His illustrated furniture catalogue made him famous around the world and both Louis XIV and Catherine the Great were known to own copies.

Not only a designer of furniture, Chippendale also made wallpaper, brassware and carpets, and his illustrious clients included the architect Robert Adam, the actor David Garrick, the outrageous Mrs Cornelys (Chippendale was one of her creditors when she was imprisoned for debt) and Lord Mansfield, who installed Chippendale's work at his Kenwood House home in Hampstead. Similarly, Lord Shelbourne bought furniture for his Lansdowne House property in Berkeley Square.

On Chippendale's death in 1779, the business passed to his sons but tastes were changing. In 1793 Chippendale's work was described as 'wholly antiquated and laid aside'. In 1804 the business failed and all the company's remaining stock was auctioned. 'Beautiful Mahogany Cabinet Work of the first class, including many articles of great taste and the finest workmanship' were sold off in under two days.

Clare Market

Aldwych

BUILT IN AN AREA PREVIOUSLY KNOWN AS ST Clement's Inn Fields, Clare Market was established in 1651 on land owned by Lord Clare, whose family home – 'a princely mansion' – once stood here.

The market was held every Wednesday and Saturday and became famous for its meat and fish. By 1850, more than twenty-five butchers were slaughtering almost 400 sheep and 200 bullocks a week. However, the gradual encroachment of

slum dwellings saw the market's reputation decline. Writing in 1881, Walter Thornbury noted that 'merchandise at present exposed for sale … consists principally of dried fish, inferior vegetables, and such humble viands, suited to the pockets of the poor inhabitants of the narrow courts and alleys around'.

The market was not to survive many more years. Much of the land on which it stood was used for the building of the Royal Courts of Justice. Today, its name is remembered in a meagre passageway on the campus of the London School of Economics.

Coldbath Fields Prison

Clerkenwell

BUILT IN 1794 ON THE SITE OF A COLD
spring discovered in 1697, this prison was
notorious for the severity of its regime.

It was immortalized by Samuel Taylor Coleridge, who wrote:
As he went through Coldbath Fields he saw a solitary cell:
And the Devil was pleased, for it gave him a hint
For improving his prisons in Hell.

The first prison governor, Thomas Aris, allowed inmates one visitor and one letter every three months. Hopes that the next governor might oversee an improvement in conditions were dashed when Aris was replaced by a military man with even harsher views. Under the guidance of George Chesterton from 1828, the prison population doubled to 1150. Many were short-term prisoners, and 10,000 petty thieves, drunks and vagrants passed through its walls every year. Chesterton did root out corruption in his staff by placing spies among them, but he also imposed a vicious regime on the prisoners, including total silence. Protesters were flogged, placed in solitary confinement wearing leg irons, and fed bread and water.

Perhaps the jail's most famous inmates were the Cato Street conspirators (led by Arthur Thistlewood), who were subsequently moved to the Tower of London before being hanged at Newgate. Coldbath Fields was closed in 1877 and

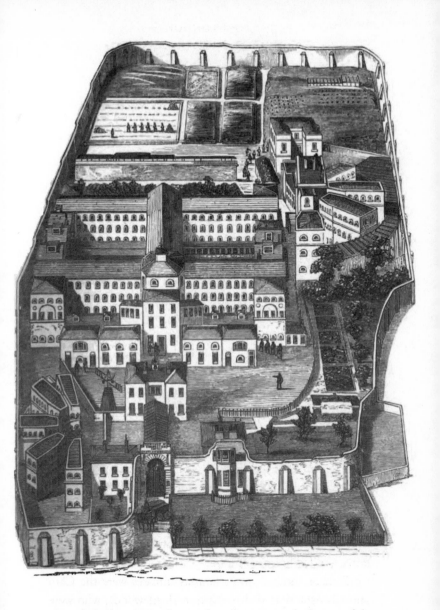

demolished in 1889, the site later becoming the home of the Mount Pleasant sorting office.

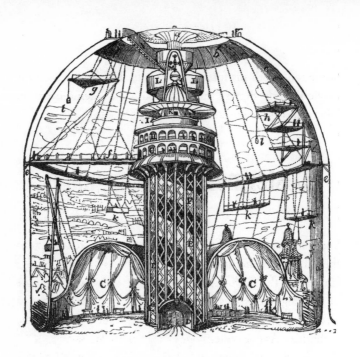

Colosseum

❧

Regent's Park

A VAST ROTUNDA BUILT IN REGENT'S PARK BY
Decimus Burton between 1824 and 1827, with a dome
very slightly larger than that of St Paul's Cathedral.

It housed a huge canvas panorama of London, painted by
Thomas Hornor. However, the attraction's initial popularity
soon waned and in 1831 the building was sold to opera
singer John Barham, whose dream to turn it into an opera

house took both his fortune and his health. Briefly used for magic-lantern shows, the Colosseum was demolished in 1872 and is now covered by Cambridge Gate.

Costermongers' Language

Today's street slang and text-speak can trace their roots back to the Victorian costermongers (street traders) who developed a language of their own. Their motives were very similar to those of the slang-merchants of today – to mark themselves out as separate and special, and to avoid being understood by the authorities. As one costermonger was reported as saying:

The Irish can't tumble it anyhow; the Jews can tumble it better … Some of the young salesmen of Billingsgate can understand us – but only at Billingsgate, and they think they are uncommon clever, but they're not quite up to the mark. The police don't understand us at all. It would be a pity if they did.

Here are a few favourite costermonger phrases:

A doogheno or badheno?	*Is it a good or bad market?*
A regular trosseno	*A regular bad one*
Cool him	*Look at him*
Cross chap	*A thief*
Do the tightner	*Going to dinner*
Doing dab	*Doing badly*
Flash it	*Show it*
Flatch kanurd	*Half-drunk*
I'm on to the deb	*Going to bed*

Kennetseeno	*Sticking*
Nomus	*Do off*
Tumble to your barrkin	*Understand you*

Crapper and Company Ltd

Chelsea

**Thomas Crapper was subject to an enduring
myth that he lent his name to a popular slang verb
(the word crap derives from the Dutch *krappe*),**

Thomas Crapper was a plumber who ran a very successful
business (on the King's Road in Chelsea) making celebrated
water closets between 1861 and the late 1920s. Crapper's
former premises at 120 King's Road is became the site the of
Dorothy Perkins store.

Cremorne Gardens

Chelsea

**A 12-acre site between The King's Road and
the River Thames, Cremorne was a Victorian
revival of an earlier pleasure gardens.**

It was originally opened as Cremorne Stadium in 1832 by Charles Random de Berenger, who styled himself Baron de Beaufain or Baron de Berenger (depending on how the mood took him). His aristocratic heritage was entirely fictitious and he had in fact only recently been released from King's Bench Prison for stockmarket fraud.

Promising 'manly exercise' including boxing, swimming, fencing, rowing and shooting, the venture was not the success that the 'Baron' had hoped. Having changed hands, it reopened in 1840 as a pleasure garden, complete with banqueting hall, theatre, bowling, grottoes and lavender bowers, and enough space to accommodate 1,500 people.

With a grand entrance on King's Road, the entry fee of one shilling permitted guests fifteen hours of entertainment, including fireworks shows, circuses and side shows. But Cremorne's speciality was balloon ascents, which became increasingly daring and dangerous and thoroughly captured the public imagination. One exponent, Charles Green, memorably made one flight in the company of a leopard. Another, 'The Flying Man' Goddard, rose to 5,000ft in his Montgolfier Fire Balloon in 1864, before drifting into the spire of St Luke's Church on nearby Sydney Street with fatal results.

By the 1870s Cremorne Gardens had acquired a poor reputation and the local Baptist minister issued a pamphlet calling it a 'nursery of every kind of vice'. Despite successfully suing for libel, the owner, John Baum, was awarded only a farthing in damages. Ruined both in health and pocket, Baum's licence was withdrawn in 1877. Lots Road power station later came to cover much of the site.

Crossing Sweepers

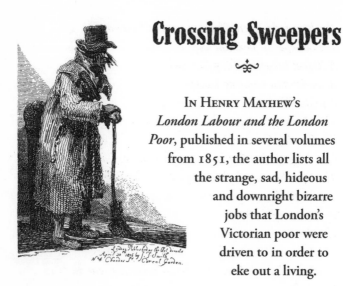

IN HENRY MAYHEW'S
*London Labour and the London
Poor*, published in several volumes
from 1851, the author lists all
the strange, sad, hideous
and downright bizarre
jobs that London's
Victorian poor were
driven to in order to
eke out a living.

He gives over almost thirty pages to the now defunct work of the crossing sweeper; who kept busy street crossings free from rubbish and horse dung in the hope of eliciting a few pence from those traversing the highway.

Many turned to this business as its start-up costs were minimal – one merely needed a broom. It provided a job that meant the sweeper would avoid being charged with begging, and if they could establish a regular pitch, they might earn the sympathy of local householders and shopkeepers and begin to make a regular income from them.

Mayhew lists a number of banks and businesses that employed crossing sweepers to keep their customers' feet clean en route to their premises. He interviewed many of them and categorized them thus:

Able-bodied Crossing Sweepers
The Aristocratic Crossing Sweeper

The Bearded Crossing Sweeper at the Exchange
The Sweeper in Portland Square
A Regent Street Crossing Sweeper
A Tradesman Crossing Sweeper
An Old Woman
The Crossing Sweeper who had been a Serving Maid
The Sunday Crossing Sweeper
One-Legged Crossing Sweeper of Chancery Lane
The Most Severely Inflicted of all the Crossing Sweepers
The Negro Crossing Sweeper who has lost both his legs
Boy Crossing Sweepers
Gander The 'Captain' of the Crossing Sweepers
The King of the Tumbler Boy Crossing Sweepers
*(And finally) The Girl Crossing Sweeper sent out by
her Father.*

The Devil Public House

Fleet Streeet

**A PUBLIC HOUSE, DATING BACK TO THE 16TH
century, whose sign depicted St Dunstan tweaking
the nose of the devil, was the site of the Apollo
Club, home to wits, writers and poets presided
over by the playwright, Ben Jonson.**

The rules of the club, most likely written by Jonson himself,
stated:

Let none but guests or clubbers hither come;
Let dunces, fools, and sordid men keep home;
Let learned, civil, merry men b' invited,
And modest, too; nor be choice liquor slighted.
Let nothing in the treat offend the guest:
More for delight than cost prepare the feast.

Other rules forbade reciting insipid poetry, fighting,
brawling, itinerate fiddlers, the discussion of serious or sacred
subjects, the breaking of glass or windows, and the tearing
down of tapestries in wantonness (presumably tearing them
down with good reason was excusable).

During Cromwell's Commonwealth, the Devil became
the favourite roost of 'Mull Sack' – so named because his
chosen drink was spiced sherry. Mull Sack's real name was
John Cottington, a sweep turned highwayman and cutpurse,
who reputedly had stolen from both the Lord Protector

Cromwell and Charles II and who was immortalized in popular ballads of the time.

In 1746 the Royal Society held its annual dinner here and during the 1750s concerts were regularly hosted. Eventually the Devil was incorporated into Child's Bank, which stands at No 1 Fleet Street.

Dioramas

A FASHIONABLE DIVERSION AND FORERUNNER OF the cinema, the first diorama opened in 1781 at Lisle Street. Described by its inventor, Philippe de Loutherbough, as 'Various imitations of Natural Phenomena represented by Moving Pictures', it consisted of a series of mechanically operated scenes, such as a storm at sea.

The most famous diorama opened in 1823 at Nos 9–10 Park Square East, Camden. In a darkened auditorium, 200 seated visitors were treated to a series of vast trompe l'oeils painted by Jacques Daguerre, inventor of the first successful photographic technique. The entire seating could be rotated through nearly ninety degrees by a boy operating a ram engine, allowing parts of a scene to be displayed while other parts were prepared off-stage and out of sight. Measuring seventy feet wide and forty feet high, the giant paintings included the interior of Canterbury Cathedral. One visitor described the experience of seeing the former thus: 'The organ peels from under some distant vaults. Then the daylight slowly returns, the congregation disperses, the candles are extinguished and the church with its chairs appears as at the beginning. This was magic.'

Although hailed as an artistic triumph, the venture was a commercial failure and in 1848 the building, its machinery and paintings were sold for £3000. The site was later converted into a Baptist chapel, though the original frontage survives.

The Dog and Duck

Southwark

A FAMOUS PUBLIC HOUSE, NAMED AFTER EITHER
the shape of the nearby ponds or the habit of
allowing dogs to chase the ducks that lived on them.

The pub gained a reputation not only for its sporting contests but also for its health-giving waters. Sold at 4d a gallon and recommended by no less a figure than Dr Johnson to his friend Mrs Thrale, the waters were advertised in 1731 as being a cure for 'rheumatism, stone, gravel, fistula, ulcers, cancers, eye sores, and in all kinds of scorbutic cases whatever, and the restoring of lost appetite'.

If healthy competition was more your thing, in 1711 the pub hosted a 'grinning match' in which contestants, to the accompaniment of music, competed for a gold-laced hat.

The Dog and Duck was much enlarged over time to include a bowling alley and an organ for popular concerts. But in contrast to the nearby Vauxhall Gardens, it gained a poor reputation, attracting as it did 'riff-raff and the scum of the town'.

Numerous highwaymen of the 18th century made mention of the pub and in 1787 it was refused a licence until the Mayor of Southwark intervened. It was again refused one in 1796, at which stage it changed from a public house into a vintners, which needed no licence to operate. It closed down altogether three years later. With the pub demolished, the site became home to St Bethlehem when it moved from Moorfield in 1811. A stone plaque from the Dog and Duck, portraying a sitting dog with a duck in its mouth and bearing the date 1617, was incorporated into its walls but was later moved to the Cuming Museum in Lambeth.

Dog Finders

ONE METHOD THAT SOME POOR LONDONERS used to earn money was the trick of 'lurking' or dog finding.

Henry Mayhew interviewed one dog finder for his great work on London, a man named Chelsea George who had been educated as a gentlemen but had fallen on hard times.

Chelsea George had a cunning technique. He would paint his hand with gelatine mixed with pulverized fried liver and then approach a dog that looked 'a likely spec'. Rubbing his hand on the animal's nose, it soon became a willing captive. He would abduct the animal with a sack he carried for the purpose, then have flyers printed declaring 'Dog Found'. He posted one at a local public house with a friendly landlord and the other he kept on his person.

When the dog's owner approached the publican, they were directed to George, who would produce the other flyer – saying he had come across it during the day – and return the dog for a reward. Mayhew believed Chelsea George had run this trick for nearly fifteen years 'without the slightest imputation on his character', earning him an annual income of around £150 (which in Victorian London put him on a par with a headmaster, and way above a labourer who could expect £25 per year).

Don Saltero's Coffee House

Chelsea

A CHELSEA INSTITUTION FOR ALMOST 150 YEARS, Don Saltero's was opened in 1695 by one James Salter, a barber and former servant of Sir Hans Sloane.

Originally on the corner of Lawrence Street, it moved first to Danvers Street and then in 1717 to Cheyne Walk This popular coffee house was packed with curiosities donated by Sloane, whose collection of objects would later form the

basis of the British Museum.

Salter acquired his 'Don' nickname from Rear-Admiral Sir John Munden a notorious lover of all things Spanish. Salter was an eccentric, not only serving his customers coffee but also shaving them, pulling their teeth, reciting poetry and playing the violin. His fame reached its apogee in 1709 when an edition of the *Tatler* was dedicated to his shop and its 'ten thousand gimcracks'.

After Salter's death in 1728, the business passed to his daughter. A year later a catalogue of the items in the coffee house was published, and again in 1795. A good many of them were sold off in 1799, raising £50 despite (or perhaps because of) including 'a starved cat found between the walls of Westminster Abbey when repairing'. No 18 Cheyne Walk, built in 1867, now sits on the site.

Durham House

The Strand

**FOR 800 YEARS BEFORE THE EMBANKMENT WAS
built, the Strand was the site of many of London's
finest houses, offering both river views and close
proximity to the City and Westminster.**

Durham House was originally built in the mid-14th century as the town house of the Bishop of Durham. The first office-holder to reside there was Richard Le Poor. Legend has it that Henry III was once passing nearby during a thunderstorm when the then incumbent, Simon de Montfort, invited him in to take refuge. The king replied, 'Thunder and lightning I fear much, but by the head of God I fear thee more'.

The house also served as home to both Cardinal Wolsey and Anne Boleyn, while Katherine of Aragon lodged here before her marriage to Henry VIII's older brother, Arthur. Lady Jane Grey was wed here on 21 May 1553, shortly before her tragic nine days on the throne of England. By the time of Elizabeth I's reign, the house was described as 'stately and high, supported with lofty marble pillars. It standeth on the Thames very pleasantly.' It eventually became the home of

Sir Walter Raleigh and while living there he was memorably drenched with beer by a servant who feared that his master had caught fire when he found him smoking.

After Raleigh's untimely eviction from the property when he fell from favour, James I used it mainly to house visiting ambassadors, although its gardens were incorporated into neighbouring Cecil House. In Oliver Cromwell's time it was used for billeting troops and in 1660, by then much dilapidated, it was demolished. Slum housing occupied the site for the next 100 years until the construction of the Adams Brothers, Adelphi Buildings in 1769. The only reminder of the original building left today is Durham House Street.

Eel Pie House

Highbury

Standing just north of Highbury Sluice, which controlled the flow of water from the New River (a man-made channel), Eel Pie House was famous not only for its pies but its tea and hot rolls too.

Although it was commonly believed that the eponymous eels were local, they were in fact imported from the Netherlands.

The pub was a hot spot for the working class from at least 1804, ideally situated for leisure pursuits and fishing. With gardens next to the 'Boarded River' aqueduct, a walk from the pie house to Hornsey Woods became a Palm Sunday tradition. Although urban development rapidly encroached, guidebooks still listed it as a popular destination as late as 1844. But within twenty years the river and the surrounding countryside were built over. The approximate site of Eel Pie House is today covered by No. 57 Wilberforce Road.

Effra River

South London

ALTHOUGH NOT TRULY LOST – HIDDEN IS A MORE appropriate word – the Effra is one of several central London rivers of which there is now almost no evidence above ground. Others include the Peck, the Fleet, the Tybourne, the Westbourne and the Walbrook.

The Effra rose in Upper Norwood and flowed through Dulwich along Croxted Road to Herne Hill, along the side of Brockwell Park, then down Brixton Road to Kennington Church, around the curve of the Oval, past what used to be Vauxhall Gardens, then into the Thames immediately above Vauxhall Bridge. History records that it was 12ft wide and 6ft deep around Brixton Road. Although it served as a sewer in Brixton from the 17th century, its waters were still being used in Dulwich as late as 1860. It provided water to the Vauxhall Water Works Company until they moved

their source of supplies outside the capital. Still visible in Dulwich's Belair Park, today the river supplies a couple of ponds before disappearing underground and linking into the sewer system.

Egyptian Hall

Piccadilly

BUILT IN AN ORNATE EGYPTIAN STYLE BY
G F Robinson in 1812 at a cost of £16,000, the
Hall housed a natural history museum based on
the collection of William Bullock, who spent thirty
years travelling in South and Central America.

Even more popular was a collection of memorabilia it hosted celebrating Napoleon Bonaparte, including his bullet-proof carriage. It drew enormous crowds totalling 800,000 in the course of a year, producing an income that could pay the building costs twice over. When the exhibits were eventually sold off, Madame Tussaud bought many of them.

In 1820 the Hall was hired by the painter Benjamin Haydon to display his enormous canvas depicting Christ's entry into Jerusalem. When it was later used to show artefacts from the tomb of Seti 1, it attracted 1800 visitors on the first day alone. As the century progressed, the Hall became ever less high-brow, coming to specialize in freak shows. Although Turner showed

EGYPTIAN HALL.
ENGLAND'S HOME OF MYSTERY.

Lessee and Manager - - Mr. J. N. MASKELYNE.

TWENTIETH CONSECUTIVE YEAR IN LONDON.
Performances TWICE DAILY, at 3 and 8.

The oldest-established and premier Magical Entertainment of the World.

ORIGINAL MAGICAL SKETCHES,
INTRODUCING
ASTOUNDING ILLUSIONS
AND SO-CALLED
SPIRITUAL MANIFESTATIONS.
AN INGENIOUS INTERWEAVING OF
REFINED FUN AND PROFOUND MYSTERY.
INIMITABLE, CONSEQUENTLY UNIQUE.

THE SENSATION OF 1892.
THE MAHATMAS OUTDONE.
A Human Being apparently disintegrated and precipitated invisibly through space whilst held by a Committee elected by the Audience.

THE MOST STARTLING MYSTERY EVER PRESENTED TO THE PUBLIC.

Fauteuils, 5s.; Reserved Seats, 3s.; Area, 2s.; Balcony, 1s.
Children Half-price (Balcony excepted). Babies, Ten Guineas each.

I

his watercolours here in 1824, one was more likely to come across Claude Amboise Seurat, a Frenchman know as 'the living skeleton'.

Later it would showcase Cheng and Eng (Siamese Twins), and in 1844 the American showman, Phineas T Barnum, took an impressive £125 a day showing off General Tom Thumb. Other highlights included a family of Laplanders complete with sledges and dogs, a three-mile-long canvas panorama of the Mississippi River and the skeleton of a mammoth. From 1852–58, Albert Richard Smith used the

Hall for over 2000 re-enactments of his ascent of Mont Blanc. The building was demolished in 1904, with an office block at Nos 170–173 now standing on the site.

Enon Chapel

Near the Strand

Opened in 1822, this Baptist chapel became notorious for a scandal that erupted in 1844 when a sewer was being constructed beneath it.

Having for many years charged cheap burial fees, the crypt beneath the chapel had long proved a popular choice among the local poor from whence to embark on the afterlife. With the sewer requiring that the chapel undergo structural alterations, the Baptist minister took the opportunity to remove some of the 'earth' building up beneath his chapel. He had the earth carried off to a new road being built on the south side of Waterloo Bridge and the alarm was raised when a human hand was discovered in one of the carts. It emerged that the church's worshippers had had only a few floor boards separating them from over 12,000 people interred in the crypt, covered by the merest scattering of earth.

The renovation works were halted and the chapel subsequently closed, to be taken over by a group of teetotallers who seemed content to hold dances and host a Sunday school just a matter of feet and inches above the corpses. The affair brought attention to the disgraceful state of many of the city's burial grounds and a Parliamentary Select Committee was established to deal with numerous overflowing sites from Aldgate to Soho. A worshipper from Enon Chapel was called to give evidence and told the committee:

At the time I attended it ... there were interments, and the place was in a very filthy state: the smell was most abominable and very injurious; I have frequently gone home with a severe headache which I supposed to have been occasioned by the smell, more particularly in the summer time; also, there were insects ... I have seen them in the summertime hundreds of them flying about the chapel; I have taken them home in my hat, and my wife has taken them home in her clothes; we always considered that they proceed from the dead bodies underneath.

The remains were finally removed in 1847 and reburied in a single pit in a cemetery in Norwood, but not before becoming something of a tourist attraction. In his 1878 work *London Old and New*, Thornbury wrote:

The work of exhumation was then commenced, and a pyramid of human bones was exposed to view, separated from piles of coffin wood in various stages of decay. This 'Golgotha' was visited by about 6000 persons, previous to its removal, and some idea may be formed of the horrid appearance of the scene, when it is stated that the quantity of remains comprised four upheaved van loads.

The London School of Economics' St Clement's Building now sits atop the former charnel house.

Essex House

Near the Strand

LOCATED ON THE CURRENT ESSEX STREET, SOUTH
of the Strand, Essex House was home to the
Bishops of Essex from the early 1300s.

In a history chequered with uprisings, the property witnessed
Walter Stapleton holding out against the rebellious city
populace here in 1326 until they stormed the gates,
plundering or burning the plate, money, jewellery and
goods contained within. Bishop Stapleton rode out on his
horse to seek sanctuary but was dragged from his saddle near
St Paul's and hauled by the mob to Cheapside, where he was
stripped and beheaded. His head was set on a pole and his
body burnt in a pile of rubbish outside his own gates.

In the 16th century, Essex House became the property
of Robert, Earl of Essex, one of Elizabeth 1's favourites.
But after a failed military campaign in Ireland, he foolishly
attempted to rouse the city against the queen. Despite being
personally popular, none of the citizenry joined his cause
and while attempting to return home, he was met by a
troop of soldiers who promptly delivered him to the Tower
of London. After being tried for treason, he was beheaded
on 25 February 1601 on Tower Hill.

His son, Robert Devereux, achieved some success as a
Parliamentarian general during the Civil War and received
a delegation from the House of Commons at Essex House

after his victory at the First Battle of Newbury in 1643. When Pepys visited Devereux's body as it lay in state in 1646, he set aside his admiration for the general to describe the mansion as 'large but ugly'. In a famous depiction of one of London's 17th century 'Frost Fairs', parts of Essex House and its gardens can be seen in the background as Charles II and the royal family walk along the ice to view the sports on offer.

The building had been divided in two in 1640, with half sold to a speculator who demolished it and laid out Essex Street in its place. For a while the remaining half of the property served as the Cotton Library of Manuscripts (now part of the British Library) but was finally demolished in 1777.

Euston Arch

WHEN EUSTON STATION WAS FIRST OPENED IN 1837, its entrance was dominated by Euston Arch, which stood 72ft high and was supported by four Doric columns to make it the largest arch in Great Britain.

Costing over £30,000, the railway board attempted to publicly justify the expense: 'The entrance to the London passenger station, opening immediately upon what will necessarily become the Grand Avenue for travelling between the Midland and Northern parts of the Kingdom, the directors thought that it should receive some embellishment.'

A hundred years later, with the Victoria and Adelaide hotels having been built either side, the arch was recognized as a major landmark and 'the most imposing entrance to a London terminus'. Some contemporaries, though, were much less forgiving. In *Old and New London*, Thornbury described it as 'a lofty and apparently meaningless Doric temple – for it seems placed without reference to the courtyard it leads to … and although handsome in itself, and possibly one of the largest porticoes in the world, it nevertheless falls far short in grandeur to the Arc de Triomphe in Paris. Some of the blocks of stone used in its construction weighed thirteen tons.'

However, when the station entrance was completely redesigned and rebuilt in 1962, the heedless demolition of the arch galvanized the nascent preservation movement. Although it failed to save the arch, many other historic buildings owe their survival to groups formed as a result. There is even talk of having the arch reconstructed as the stone work itself was saved to make a bed for the channels of Bow Backs River, which occupies the Lea Valley.

Execution Dock

Wapping

A mile downstream from the Tower of London at the Wapping bend of the Thames was a jumble of houses and wharves known as Execution Dock.

For 400 years from the time of Henry VI, condemned pirates met their fate at this site and, in contrast to executions at Tyburn, once they were dead they were not immediately cut down. As John Stow explained, they were left 'to remain till three tides had overflowed them'. The condemned were often housed at the Marshalsea Prison before being taken by boat to Wapping to be hung close to the water's edge at low tide.

Throngs of sightseers would attend on land and on the water, and there were still more degradations for these high-seas highwaymen. To discourage others, their bodies were often covered in tar to preserve them from the weather and to prevent birds pecking out their softer parts. Their corpses were then hung in chains – gibbetted – along various points on the river.

The notorious English privateer, Captain Kidd, was hanged here on 23 May 1701. During his execution, the hangman's rope broke and Kidd had to be strung up again. His body was then gibbeted and remained a landmark by the river for the next 20 years. The Captain Kidd pub in Wapping continues to keep his name alive. George Davis and William Watts were the final victims to hang at the dock on 16 December 1830. John Rocque's 1746 map of the capital marks Execution Dock as being near the modern day Wapping Tube Station.

Exeter House

The Strand

ANOTHER OF THE GREAT STRAND MANSIONS,
built in the reign of Edward VI (1547–1553) for
Sir Thomas Palmer, who was executed in 1553.
Elizabeth I later gifted the house to William Cecil.

When she subsequently visited here, she graciously allowed him to sit, rather than stand, in her presence as he was suffering from gout at the time. 'My lord,' she is reputed to have told her Lord Treasurer, 'we make use of you not for the badness of your legs, but for the goodness of your head.'

The house was badly damaged in a fire and was rebuilt in 1627. After the Great Fire of 1666, it hosted the Admiralty Court, the Prerogative Court and Court of Arches until the Doctors Commons could be repaired. Exeter House was demolished once and for all in the 1670s, with Exeter Change built in its place. This was intended to be a thriving marketplace, with space for a variety of small shops, but it never took off. It was rented as office space until it was taken over by Edward Cross, who housed his famous menagerie here from 1773 prior to its move to Surrey Gardens.

Byron famously compared Cross's hippos to the then Prime Minister, Lord Liverpool. Another of the most popular exhibits was a five-ton elephant called Chunee, who one day ran amok and had to be killed by its keeper with a harpoon after several failed attempts to halt the animal with gunfire and canon. Nine butchers flayed the animal – a job that took twelve hours – before ten surgeons dissected the body in front of an audience of medical students.

The menagerie was closed and the Change demolished in 1829, to be re-built between 1829 to 1831 as Exeter Hall. It was used by the Ragged School Union, the Sacred Harmonic Society, the Temperance Society and the Bible Society, and even received a visit from Prince Albert for a series of lectures conducted by the anti-slavery movement. It was ultimately taken over by the YMCA but was knocked down in 1907 and replaced by the Strand Palace Hotel.

Farringdon Market

※

OPENED ON 20 NOVEMBER 1829 TO REPLACE
Fleet Market – which had been closed after the
widening of Farringdon Road – Farringdon
Market traded fruit and vegetables and was
designed to serve a middle-class clientele.

However, built at a cost of nearly a quarter of a million
pounds, it quickly failed to live up to its owners' aspirations.
In his 1878 work *London Old and New*, Thornbury reported:

*Its produce, however, is very humble, and rarely rises
above the rank of the modest onion, the plebeian cabbage,
the barely respectable cauliflower, the homely apple, and other
unpretending fruits and vegetables. Pineapples and hot-house
grapes are unknown to its dingy sheds.*

The market became the resort of the poorest-of-the-
poor traders, with receipts from the Common Council

showing an average annual income from the hire of stalls of just £225.

Henry Mayhew, who visited one cold, November morning, recalled:

As the morning twilight drew on, the paved court was crowded with customers. The sheds and shops at the end of the market grew every moment more distinct, and a railway van, laden with carrots, came rumbling into the yard. The pigeons, too, began to fly into the sheds, or walk about the paving-stones, and the gas-man came round with his ladder to turn out the lamps. Then every one was pushing about, the children crying as their naked feet were trodden upon, and the women hurrying off with their baskets or shawls filled with cresses, and the bunch of rushes in their hands. In one corner of the market, busily tying up their bunches, were three or four girls, seated on the stones, with their legs curled up under them, and the ground near them was green with the leaves they had thrown away. A saleswoman, seeing me looking at the group, said, 'Ah, you should come here of a summer's morning, and then you'd see 'em, sitting tying up, young and old, upwards of a hundred poor things, as thick as crows in a ploughed field.

However, Farringdon Market was the place to go for watercress, with upwards of twenty tons sold each week. Hundreds of retailers – men, women, girls and boys – would arrive here at 3am every day to sell cress by the hand. With the amount to be sold dependent on the size of the trader's fist, the call of 'Don't pinch your hand, governor' was regularly to be heard from the buyers of Farringdon.

The market relocated in 1883 to Smithfield, though for many years booksellers continued to congregate on Farringdon Road.

Fauconberg House

Soho

STANDING ON THE NORTHEAST CORNER OF
Soho Square, (also home to the equally famous
Monmouth House) this was the home of Thomas
Belasyse, First Earl of Fauconberg (1627–1700).

Originally from a Royalist family, he married one of Oliver
Cromwell's daughters but swapped sides again at the
Restoration in 1660, only to betray James II and invite William
III to take the English throne in the Glorious Revolution of
1688, an act for which he received his earldom.

The famously cross-eyed Speaker of the House of
Commons, Arthur Onslow, made Fauconberg House his
residence from 1753 to 1761. The building was improved by
Robert Adam and went on to serve as Wright's Hotel and
Coffee House for almost fifty years until 1857, at which point
it was taken over by an instrument-maker. In 1858 Crosse
& Blackwell opened a pickle-bottling plant on the premises,
which the company later turned into offices and a five-storey
factory producing soups, chutneys and marmalades to sell
across the British Empire. With the building demolished in
the 1920s to make way for the Astoria Cinema, only the dreary
and rarely noticed Falconberg Mews remains as a reminder.
The whole area was swept away to make room for the capital's
massive Crossrail development in 2010.

Field of the Forty Footsteps

Russell Square

IN 1685, THE YEAR OF THE MONMOUTH REBELLION,
it is said that two brothers, both courting the same
woman, fought a duel for her affections in the fields
behind Montague House (now the British Museum).

Both died from their resulting wounds and from that day
forward, so the legend goes, no grass would grow in the
footsteps where they trod, or on the tussock where the girl at
the centre of the dispute sat to watch the contest.

A letter addressed to the poet Robert Southey (1774–
1843) from his friend John Walsh encouraged Southey to visit
the Fields:

*I think it would be worth your while to take a view of
those wonderful marks of the Lord's hatred to duelling called
'The Brothers' Steps.' They are in a field about a third of a mile
northward from Montague house ... The prints of their feet are
about the depth of three inches, and nothing will vegetate them
so much as to disfigure them ... Mr. George Hall, who was the
Librarian of Lincoln's Inn, first showed me these steps twenty-
eight years ago ... he remembered them about thirty years, and
the man who first showed them to him about thirty more, which
goes back to the year 1692 ... My mother well remembered their
being ploughed up and corn sown to displace them, about fifty
years ago, but all was labour in vain, for the prints returned in a
while to their pristine form.*

The exact location of the site is debated, with some arguing for the car park behind Senate House on the west of Russell Square while others suggest an area in front of Birkbeck College, slightly to the north. Fanciful visitors might still glimpse footprints in the grass newly laid there, though students taking short-cuts across the lawn might be a more logical cause.

Fleet Marriages

BETWEEN 1617 AND 1753 A LEGAL LOOPHOLE meant that on-the-spot marriages could be carried out in an area surrounding the Fleet Debtors' Prison known as the 'Liberties of the Fleet'.

Many of the pubs nearby bore the sign of a happy couple holding hands, alongside a caption: 'Marriages performed within'. Often the ceremonies were conducted by clergymen incarcerated in the Fleet for debt. It was widely believed by the ruling classes that many of these marriages were forced and nothing but a sham. The image of a drunken son of the aristocracy reeling down the street in the arms of a lady of ill-repute was much bandied about and angry voices were raised in Parliament on the matter.

Indeed, no doubt some illicit matches did take place, against the will of one or other of the parties. But judging from the number of unions made (estimated to be almost 250,000 in just sixty years up to 1753), it seems more likely that the ability to marry without parental consent – that is to say, to marry who you wanted, rather than who they wanted – might well have been the commoner motivation. Records show that in the four months up to 12 February 1705 alone, almost 3,000 marriages took place.

The Liberties of the Fleet in many ways resembled Las Vegas of today, a notorious area famed for debauchery and where the reach of the law was restricted. A campaign led by Lord Hardwicke eventually resulted in the Marriage Act of 1753, which finally put an end to the practise in England and Wales.

Fleet Prison

Blackfriars

STANDING ON THE EAST BANK OF THE FLEET
River on the site of the current Blackfriars Railway
Station, this prison was first recorded in 1171. The
office of Keeper was a hereditary post handed down
through the Leveland family from 1197 to 1538.

The job offered opportunity for hideous abuses, with the Keeper entitled to raise levies on prisoners for almost everything, from food and lodging to privileges. Inmates could also pay to be released for short periods and many escaped.

Very unpopular among the public, the prison was burnt down during both the Peasants' Revolt of 1381 and the Gordon Riots of 1780. In between, it was ravaged by the 1666 Great Fire of London. Although nominally a debtors' prison, the Fleet was used in the 14th century to incarcerate those condemned by the King's Council and the Court of Chancery, as well as those convicted by the Court of the Star Chamber between Henry VIII's reign and 1641.

In 1691 a prisoner named Moses Pitt wrote *Cry of the Oppressed* about his experiences at Fleet, in which he revealed the full extent of his degradations. Instead of the regulation 4s flat fee, he was charged £2 4s 6D to be housed in the 'gentleman's side' and paid a further 8s a week for his room. Having run out of money after sixteen months, he was thrown in a dungeon to sleep on the floor with twenty-seven other inmates 'so lowsie, that as they either walked or sat down, you might have pick'd lice off from their outward garments'.

A Parliamentary inquiry in 1726 found the then Keeper, Thomas Bambridge, guilty 'of great extortions, and the highest crimes and misdemeanours in the execution of his said office', treating prisoners 'in a most barbarous and cruel manner'. New rules were imposed but in reality little changed for the unfortunates held at Fleet. Charles Dickens described in vivid detail life within its walls in the 1830s in *The Pickwick Papers*. The prison was closed in 1842 and demolished four years later.

Fleet River

Although the Fleet River has entirely disappeared from above ground, its source is still visible and, weather permitting, you may even swim in it still.

It rises in Hampstead Heath and fills the ponds from Kenwood House down through the heath towards Kentish Town (a name possibly derived from 'Ken Ditch Town'). The Fleet's upper reaches were long famed for their health-giving waters, though the same could not be said for its lower reaches.

The river's ancient valley followed the route of Kentish Town Road, then St Pancras Way, Kings Cross Road, Phoenix Place and Warner Street, before joining Farringdon Road and Farringdon Street, then flowing into the Thames at Blackfriars. The Fleet marked the western limit of the Roman city boundaries and was deep enough for navigation as far as Holbourne Bridge until the 1500s, when it fell foul of rapid urban expansion and a population explosion.

The once-proud river turned into little more than a repellent ditch blocked with filth, offal and blood, though time and again the city authorities tried to restore the Fleet to its former glory. Under Queen Elizabeth 1 and then Lord Protector Cromwell, it was scoured and cleaned. In the aftermath of the 1666 Great Fire it was able to be used for the transportation of coal barges but by the early 1700s it was again in trouble. Jonathan Swift wrote of it:

Sweepings from butchers' stalls, dung, guts, and blood,
Drown'd puppies, stinking sprats, all drench'd in mud,
Dead cats, and turnip-tops, come tumbling down the flood.

The Fleet's death knell sounded when it was turned into a sewer from Fleet Bridge (at the junction of Ludgate Hill and Fleet Street) all the way to Holbourne Bridge. Stretches of the sewer remained uncovered until 1768, despite the death of a drunken Kentish barber in 1763 who was found stuck fast and frozen solid in its filthy waters. The northern part of the river was gradually covered over as the surrounding land was given over to housing projects over the course of several years.

By 1850 the Fleet was one of London's main sewers, moving 1,500,000 cubic feet of sewage per day. Its Thames-side entrance was a popular ingress into the sewer system for toshers, who made their living by sifting the dirt for anything remotely useful or valuable. 'A more dismal pursuit can scarcely be conceived' wrote John Archer in 1851 in *Vestiges of Old London*. In 1855 the Fleet was incorporated into the city's main sewage system and diverted to Barking Creek. Its name lives on in Fleet Street, Fleet Lane and in the notorious Fleet Prison.

Frost Fairs

WHEN THE WEATHER WAS SEVERE ENOUGH
that the River Thames froze over, the people of
London would take advantage and build stalls and
booths along the ice for an impromptu fair.

There are numerous records of these events that describe how pretty much anything normally available to buy on the streets was for sale on the ice, too. One contemporary sketch of an ice fair depicts signs for shops and stalls including 'the Duke of York's Coffee-house', 'the Tory booth', 'the Half-way House', 'the Bear Gardenshire Booth', 'the Roast Beef Booth', 'the Music Booth', 'the Printing Booth', 'the Lottery Booth' and 'the Horn Tavern Booth'.

Other attractions included football matches, skating, sledging and ice-based fairground games, such as a whirling-chair or a car drawn by several men using a long rope fastened to a stake fixed in the ice. Bear- and bull-baiting were also commonplace, as was the sight of a whole ox roasting, a ritual carried out with some ceremony. In 1715, one Mr Hodgeson claimed the right to dispatch an ox for the purpose – his father having performed the same task in 1684 – and arrived 'dressed in a rich laced cambric apron, a silver steel, and a hat and feathers, to perform the office'.

It is believed that there were ice fairs on the Thames in the following years: 1150, 1281, 1408, 1435, 1506, 1514, 1537, 1565, 1595, 1608, 1621, 1635, 1649, 1655, 1663, 1666, 1677, 1684, 1695, 1709, 1716, 1740, 1776, 1788,

1795 and 1814. The ice appealed to members of all classes, too. Elizabeth I was reported to have gone walking on the impromptu rink one year, while Charles II even went fox hunting on it during the great frost of 1685–6.

Printers, meanwhile, would set up stalls selling mementos of the occasion. One such included the following lines of descriptive verse:

There you may also this hard frosty winter
See on the rocky ice a Working-Printer,
Who hopes by his own art to reap some gain
Which he perchance does think he may obtain.
Here also is a lottery, music too,
Yea, a cheating, drunken, lewd, and debauch'd crew;
Hot codlins, pancakes, ducks, and goose, and sack,
Rabbit, capon, hen, turkey, and a wooden jack.

The frosts that ushered in the fairs were not without their hardships, however. The price of food and fuel would inevitably go up while as many as 3,000 people who normally earned a living ferrying goods and people along the Thames found themselves without work. The eventual break-up of the river ice caused new havoc, damaging property and taking both lives and livelihoods. In 1739, for instance, the big freeze resulted in many boats being crushed and smashed, causing damage estimated at over £100,000, while on 6 February 1815 two young men are known to have drowned. Ice also frequently carried away integral parts of London Bridge.

Gaiety Theatre

The Strand

Built where Catherine Street meets the Strand, the Gaiety Theatre opened on 21 December 1868 after the demolition of its predecessor, the Strand Music Hall.

The Gaiety was run by Lionel Lawson, owner of the *Daily Telegraph,* who wanted to create a theatre and restaurant despite laws demanding that the two businesses be separated.

The Gaiety established two firsts in British theatre – it boasted the first electrically-lighted signage on its frontage and was the first theatre to offer matinee performances. Under the management of journalist John Hollingshead and with a quick turn-around of shows, it enjoyed great success with a mixture of drama, farce and (most effectively) burlesque.

The theatre's heyday of musical comedies followed a take-over by George Edwards, with shows such as *Gaiety Girls* (1893) and *Shop Girl* (1894) proving hugely popular. A crowd of supposedly aristocratic hangers-on, besotted by the performers, came to be known as the Gaiety Girls and the Stage Door Johnnies.

The original Gaiety closed in 1903 as part of the scheme to widen the Strand, but the New Gaiety opened on 26 October that year at the corner of the Aldwych and the Strand, though with its audience capacity reduced from 2000 to 1338. It was nonetheless a wildly successful enterprise, and two of its longest running productions were Theodore and Co. (1916) and *Going Up* (1918), which featured Ivor Novello's first musical score. Both shows recorded over 500 performances each. Demolished in 1957, the theatre gave way to a spectacularly ugly office building for Citibank, which featured a blue plaque incorrectly dating the Gaiety's closure to 1938, until the offices themselves were demolished.

Gamages

High Holborn

OPENED WITH JUST 5FT OF STORE FRONTAGE in 1878 on High Holborn, Gamages grew into a successful department store. It was founded by Arthur Walter Gamage, a farmer's son who trained as a draper.

After his first year of trading he had turned over £1,632, which he used to expand his premises into the surrounding buildings. The motto that hung over the door read 'Tall oaks from little acorns grow'. It could not have been more appropriate, for the store would eventually become a veritable labyrinth, full of twists and turns and flights of steps. To give an idea of the extent of its stock, in 1911 Gamage published a mail-order catalogue running to 900 pages.

Apart from being the official supplier to the Boy Scout movement, the 'People's Popular Emporium' sold everything from pets and cars to haberdashery, furniture, gardening equipment, and sports and camping gear. Forty-nine pages of the 1911 catalogue were given over to cycles and cycling goods alone. But for children, the toy department offered the greatest delights, as Charles Spencer recalled in *A Trip to Gamages*:

Gamages was THE toy store. Every child would look forward to a visit there. Families from all over the place would take buses to High Holborn. The kids would jump off the bus with glee and dance along the street with excitement in the direction of the store

... for here they would be presented with floor upon floor of all the toys fit to see and all the toys fit to buy. Gamages was an Aladdin's cave just waiting to be discovered.

When Gamage died in 1930, he lay in state in the store before his funeral at St Andrew's, Holborn. His shop was sold in 1970 and closed in March 1972, to be redeveloped into a vast office block at a cost of £20 million.

The Gentleman's Magazine

Produced out of St John's Gate (a poor likeness of which it carried on its front covers), this was the first publication to use the word 'magazine' in reference to itself.

It was founded in 1731 by a printer, Edward Cave, and provided a monthly digest of London news and parliamentary reports for those unable to get hold of a daily newspaper – which was almost everyone who lived more than a few miles outside the city. It went through a series of name changes, being originally known as *The Gentleman's Magazine or Monthly Intelligencer*, only to replace *Monthly Intelligencer* with *Historical Chronicle* and then *Historical Review*, before finally settling on simply *The Gentleman's Magazine*.

The title ran for almost 200 years, keeping the gent-about-town up-to-date about the latest fashion trends and reading materials, as well as all the gossip he may have missed when he was away from the capital. Typically, an issue might contain an article on astronomy and another on the restoration of old paintings, a selection of Latin verse, the latest stock market prices, a list of promotions among the armed forces, clergy and legal professions, as well as the records of births and marriages plus the Bills of Mortality and obituaries.

Cave got around certain restrictions on the reporting of House of Commons debates by styling articles as the 'proceedings in the senate of Great Lilliput' – a knowing nod to Jonathan Swift's recently published satire, *Gulliver's Travels*. Dr Samuel Johnson gained his first employment as a journalist for the magazine. Other famous contributors included Oliver Goldsmith and David Garrick. By the late 1850s it had become something of an anachronism and rather unfashionable but staggered on into the 20th century, publishing its last full issue in 1907.

The Globe

Bankside

CONSIDERING THAT IT IS PERHAPS THE MOST FAMOUS theatre in the world, the original Globe had a surprisingly short, though highly eventful, existence.

It was built by the Lord Chamberlain's Men, a company of actors that included among its number the most famous playwright of them all, William Shakespeare.

Constructed entirely from wood, the theatre opened in

1599 and for the next fourteen years served as Shakespeare's base. During this time he wrote many of his greatest works, including *The Winter's Tale, The Tempest, The Merry Wives of Windsor, Measure for Measure, As You Like it, All's Well That Ends Well, Anthony and Cleopatra, Hamlet, King Lear, Macbeth* and *Othello*. Although the theatre owes its enduring fame to this association, by the time that the Globe was destroyed in a fire on 29 June 1613, Shakespeare had already sold his share of the business and retired to Stratford-upon-Avon.

A letter written by Sir Henry Wotton on 2 July 1613 gives a colourful description of the inferno that burnt the theatre to the ground:

The Kings Players had a new play, called All is True, *representing some of the principal pieces of the reign of Henry VIII, which set forth with many extraordinary circumstances of pomp and majesty even to the matting on the stage … Now King Henry making a masque at the Cardinal Wolsey's House, certain canons being shot off at his entry, some of the paper or other stuff, wherewith one of them was stopped, it did light the thatch, where, being thought at first but idle smoak, and their eyes more attentive to the show, it kindled inwardly, and ran round like a train, consuming within less than an hour the whole house to the very ground. This was the fatal period of that virtuous fabrick, wherein yet nothing did perish but wood and straw, and only a few forsaken cloaks: only one man had his breeches set on fire, that would have broiled him, if he had not, by the benefit of a provident wit, put it out with a bottle of ale.*

And that was the end of Shakespeare's Globe. A new theatre was built in 1614, on the same plans and with the aid of King James 1, and survived until the Civil War, at which point all plays were banned by the Puritan parliament. The theatre was thus demolished in 1644.

Goodman's Fields Theatre

Whitechapel

**THE NAME OF TWO INSTITUTIONS THAT HAD A
profound effect on 18th-century theatre.**

The original was opened in 1727 by Thomas Odell, deputy Licenser of Plays and himself a playwright, in a converted shop in Leman Street, Whitechapel. He had hoped to draw customers away from the West End but after a sermon was preached against him, Odell sold out to his leading actor, Henry Giffard. In 1732 Giffard opened a second premises under the same name, just around the corner in Ayliffe Street.

Edward Sheppard, architect of the Royal Opera House, was the designer of what was reported to be 'an entirely new, beautiful convenient theatre' where 'dramatic pieces were performed with the utmost elegance and propriety'. However, Giffard's decision to stage *A Vision of The Golden Rump* directly led to the passing of the 1737 Licensing Act that banned any play criticizing the government or the crown. As a result, the theatre closed but Giffard came up with a ruse to get around the new legislation.

He hit upon staging musical concerts for which entry was charged, with plays performed during the interval. The theatre reopened in 1740 and, in January 1741, revived *The Winter's Tale* for the first time in a hundred years. Giffard's next coup, and his most enduring contribution to English theatre, was to give the title role in *Richard III* to David Garrick, spuriously claiming that it was Garrick's stage debut. Despite that fib, Garrick was an instant hit, with Horace Walpole writing that 'all the run is after Garrick, at Goodman's Fields'. But political pressure from the established theatres in Lincoln's Inn and Covent Garden led to Goodman's compulsory closure on 27 May 1742 – the very day after Walpole had written those words to a friend – and it was never to reopen.

Gore House

Kensington

**Situated on the site where the
Royal Albert Hall now resides, Gore House
was built in the late 18th century.**

It was once the home of the famous anti-slavery campaigner,
William Wilberforce, before the lease was taken over by the
Countess of Blessington in the 1830s. The countess, an Irish
writer famed for her beauty and wit, worked with her son-
in-law, Count d'Orsay, to develop the house into the leading
literary salon of its day. With eminent visitors including
Disraeli, Wellington, Louis Napoleon. Walter Savage Landor
and a youthful Charles Dickens, Blessington adopted an
extravagant lifestyle that ultimately led to financial disaster.
She and the Count were ultimately forced to flee to Paris,
where she died of apoplexy in 1849.

A subsequent sale of goods from Gore House lasted 12
days and attracted vast crowds of sightseers. H H Madden,
one of Blessington's friends, visited during the sale:

*The well-known library saloon, in which the conversaziones
took place, was crowded – but not with guests… People as they
passed through the room poked the furniture, pulled apart the
precious objects of art and ornaments that lay on the table. And
some made jests. It was the most signal ruin of an establishment
I ever witnessed.*

The house briefly became a flamboyant restaurant run by

the former Reform Club chef, Alexis Soyer, but the business failed after just five months and the building was bought by the Royal Commission ahead of the 1851 Great Exhibition and demolished.

The Great Globe

Leicester Square

MAP-MAKER, GEOGRAPHER TO QUEEN VICTORIA
and MP for Bodmin, James Wyld masterminded
the Great Globe that stood in a building in
Leicester Square Gardens from 1851 to 62.

Although originally conceived as part of the Great Exhibition, the Exhibition's organizing committee ultimately deemed it too big to fit into the Crystal Palace in Hyde Park. Nonetheless, after frantic negotiations with the landlord of the Leicester Square Gardens, Wyld's scheme was hastily put into action and opened in time for the Exhibition in May 1851.

Once completed, the globe was the largest that had ever been constructed, measuring 40ft wide and 60ft high. Its interior walls featured a plaster-of-Paris scale relief of the world, with each inch representing ten miles. It was lit by gas and could be viewed from any of four stages, while 'the walls of the circular passages were hung with the finest maps, and atlases, globes and geographical works'. It was all housed in a grand, domed building in the centre of the gardens, which were once described by Charles Dickens as a 'howling wasteland … with broken railings, a receptacle for dead cats and every kind of abomination'. The attraction was an immediate success, with some 1.2 million people estimated to have visited in 1851 alone, including Prince Albert, the Duke of Wellington and the King of Belgium.

However, the closure of the Great Exhibition marked a sharp decline in both interest and visitor numbers. It further lost out to competing educational shows in Leicester Square, such as the Panopticon of Science and Arts and Burford's Panorama. By the late 1850s, Wyld himself was giving lectures inside the globe in a bid to keep it viable, but when his lease expired and he was threatened with legal action, the globe was speedily demolished and sold for scrap. Wyld reneged on his promise to return the gardens to a decent state and it was several more years before Leicester Square would lose its insalubrious reputation.

Gunter's Tea Shop

Mayfair

OPENED IN 1757 AS THE POT AND PINE APPLE by an Italian pastry chef, Domenico Negri, at 7–8 Berkeley Square, this shop specialized in 'making and selling all sorts of English, French and Italian wet and dry sweetmeats'.

Expanding to serve ice creams and sorbets too (said to be made from a secret recipe), it became a Mayfair institution and a favourite haunt of the fashionable. It was taken over by Robert Gunter in 1799, who renamed it accordingly, and won a reputation as one of a few locations where a lady could meet a gentleman without a chaperone. In those socially delicate times, coaches would park beneath the trees of Berkeley Square, the ladies sitting inside while their attentive gentlemen stood on the pavement. Waiters would take their orders and bring the famed ices out to them, dodging the traffic as they did so.

Jane Carlyle, a Victorian lady of letters and wife of historian Thomas, was recommended to visit by Charles Darwin in August 1843. She reported that he told her that she 'looked as if I needed to go to Gunter's and have an ice', an experience that she confirmed left her 'considerably revived'. The other house speciality was elaborately decorated, multi-tiered wedding cakes, an essential for every society wedding.

Gunter founded a catering and sweet-selling empire that stayed in his family for many generations and funded the construction of a large family home in Earl's Court, affectionately known as 'Currant Jelly Hall'. Redevelopment of Berkeley Square in 1936–7 saw the teashop move to Curzon Street, where it remained until 1956, the catering side of the business eventually folding twenty years later.

Hanover Square Rooms

OPENED IN 1774 AT THE CORNER OF HANOVER
Square and Hanover Street, for a century this was
one of London's premier venues for musical concerts.

Run on a subscription basis, the 800-seat concert hall was decorated with the works of Thomas Gainsborough, Benjamin West and Giovanni Battista Cipriani.

Johann Christian Bach and Karl Frederick Abel both held wildly successful seasons here and among the venue's biggest fans was George III, who had a special room laid out (the Queen's Tea Room). He even donated a large mirror to the establishment. From 1785 until 1848, *The Messiah* was performed here annually, and between 1791 and 1795 Haydn conducted a series of twelve symphonies especially written in celebration of London. From 1833 to 1866 the Philharmonic Concerts were held here and from 1846 it served as home to the Amateur Music Society.

Balls and masques were also hosted regularly, thrown by some of the most famous dandies of their day, such as Lord Alvanley, Henry Pierrepoint, Sir Henry Mildmay and Beau Brummel. One such event gave rise to one of the great put-downs of the age. Having been forced to invite the Prince Regent despite being on opposite sides of the political fence, when Brummel saw the Prince he cried out, 'Alvanley, who's your fat friend?' The Prince was apparently cut to the quick by the unerring accuracy of the barbed question.

The very last musical performance given at the Rooms was

on Saturday, 19 December 1874. The following year it was turned into a gentleman's club – The Hanover Square Club – which lasted until 1900, when the building was demolished.

Harringay Stadium

IN 1927 THIS BECAME THE THIRD GREYHOUND racing stadium to open in the country after Manchester (1926) and White City (1927). It had a capacity of 50,000, mostly on banked terracing, and a reputation for violence, with at least three major incidents garnering national attention.

In 1946, for instance, *The Guardian* reported that, following a disqualification, spectators 'invaded the track and for over half an hour indulged in senseless destruction. They started bonfires which they fed with pieces of the hare trap ... smashed electric lamps and arc lights, tore down telephone wires, and broke windows, wrecked the inside of the judge's box, overturned the starting trap ... They also attacked the tote offices.'

The involvement of gangsters was also a fact of life at the stadium and it is said that Joe Coral, founder of the famous bookmakers, was forced to resort to threatening a local gang boss, Darby Sabini, with a gun to deter the mob from taking a slice of his income. But Harringay's most extraordinary incident involved an attempt to introduce cheetah racing to the public.

On Saturday, 11 December 1937, twelve Kenyan cheetahs, which had been trained and acclimatized in Harringay, were raced in front of a packed house in Romford, Essex. The venture, though, was not a success, with the cheetahs losing interest in the competition after covering only a short distance.

Harringay was also used for speedway and stockcar racing but a decline in popularity led to the stadium closing for good and being sold to the supermarket chain, Sainsbury's, for £10 million in 1987. Some of its banked terracing can still be seen in the supermarket car park.

Highbury Barn

FAMOUS SINCE 1740 FOR ITS CREAM CAKES, IN the period 1770–1818 Highbury Barn was extended to include a bowling green and supper rooms under the management of the Willoughby family.

As host of the annual Licensed Victuallers' dinner in the 1840s, the Barn could seat 3000 diners at a time, more than twice the population of the village of Highbury itself.

Becoming known as 'The Cremorne of the North', the addition of an enormous raised, outdoor dance floor covering 4000 square ft won the venue renewed popularity. Known as 'the Leviathan', the floor was lit by huge gas globes and its advertising literature boasted that it had 'half a million lights'. It was to become the spiritual home of 'La Varsovana', a dance somewhere between a waltz and a polka.

In 1861, under the management of Edward Giovanelli, the venue was further extended to cover over five acres.

Acts who performed there included Giovanelli himself, a noted comedian, as well as famous hire-wire acts including Blondin and acrobats such as Léotard. There was also the spectacle of balloon ascents, a thriving music hall scene and novelties such as the appearance of the original Siamese twins. However, an increasingly rowdy and down-market clientele brought trouble to the Barn. In 1869, for instance, there was a notable riot by students from St Bart's that had sections of Victorian society up in arms.

In 1865 James Inches Hillocks, author of *My Life and Labours in London, A Step Nearer the Mark*, described the scene at the Barn one Sunday evening, the most popular night for visiting:

Not far distant is a band of young men, varying from fifteen to thirty years of age. They are arm in arm, occupying the entire breadth of the road. Each one is more or less intoxicated, so much so, that it requires the combined efforts of the whole to keep some of them from measuring their length upon the ground. Their conversation is of the rudest kind, and spoken in the most boisterous manner. Utterly regardless of the effects of a gross outrage on the most common sense of propriety, not to mention the higher claims of the Lord's-day, they sing. 'The Strand, the Strand,' is the song in which they all join as they marched along.

A scandalous exhibition of French dancing by the Colonna Troupe led to the Barn losing its licence in 1871. By 1883 it had been completely built over. Today, 26 Highbury Park (the Highbury Tavern) covers a tiny part of the original site.

Hippodrome Racecourse

Ladbroke Grove

HOPING THAT ITS PROXIMITY TO LONDON WOULD
draw punters from the racecourse at Epsom
Downs, in 1836 John Whyte leased 140 acres of
Ladbroke Grove for a period of twenty years.

Laying out a track for both flat-racing and steeplechasing, he
blocked the way of an ancient footpath that offered the shortest
route between Kensington Village and Kensal Green. It was a
decision that came at a heavy cost to him.

On the course's opening day in June 1837, hundreds of
visitors forced their way on to the course, successfully demanding
free entry under the terms of right of way. The *Sunday Times*
recorded that:

*A more filthy or disgusting crew than that which entered,
we have seldom had the misfortune to encounter ... relying upon
their numbers, they spread themselves over the whole of the
ground, defiling the atmosphere as they go, and carrying into the
neighbourhood of the stands and carriages, where the ladies are
most assembled, a coarseness and obscenity of language as repulsive
to every feeling of manhood as to every sense of common decency.*

Not even the racing proved successful:

*Save Hokey Pokey, there was nothing that could climb, or
hobble, much more leap over a hedge, and as to a hurdle, it was
absurd to attempt one.*

After a redesign to accommodate the public footpath, the

Hippodrome eventually reopened, with additional attractions including balloon ascents, archery and a cricket ground. At this point Whyte discovered another, fatal flaw in his plans. The course's heavy clay soil was unsuitable for horse racing. With London's rapid westward expansion, the land was in great demand for house-building. Whyte cut his losses and the last meet was held on 4 June 1841.

Hockley-in-the-Hole

Clerkenwell

IN THE REIGN OF ELIZABETH I, THE BEAR GARDENS pub at Hockley-in-the-Hole, which is located on what is today Ray Street, Clerkenwell, rivalled the Southwark Bear Gardens as a venue for dog fights, cock fights, bear- and bull-baiting.

Before fights, the animals were paraded through the streets to the beating of drums, as handbills were distributed describing the events of the day. One bill, for instance, read:

This is to give notice to all gentlemen gamesters, and others, that on this present Monday is a match to be fought by two dogs, one from Newgate Market against one from Honey Lane Market, at a Bull, for a guinea to be spent, five Let-goes out of hand; which goes fairest and farthest in wins all. Likewise a green bull to be baited, which was never baited before, and a bull to be turned loose, with fireworks all over him; also a mad ass to be baited. With a variety of bull-baiting and bear-baiting, and a dog to be drawn up with fireworks. To begin exactly at three of the clock.

Perhaps inevitably, some of the animals' keepers met with tragic accidents. Christopher Preston, for instance, was attacked and almost devoured by one of his bears in 1709.

The first advertisement for human-based 'entertainment' at Hockley-in-the-Hole dates to 1700, when the *Daily Post* reported that four men were 'to fight at sword for a bet of half-a-guinea, and six to wrestle for three pairs of gloves, at half-a-crown each pair. The entertainment to begin exactly at three o'clock.' By then, Hockley was widely regarded as a place of ill repute. Jonathan Wilde, the self-styled 'Thief-Taker General' who was executed in 1725, is thought to have lived here for a time. For many years, the Bear Gardens also displayed a suitcase inscribed 'R Turpin' and said to have belonged to the notorious highwayman.

Hockley-in-the-Hole's popularity waned as a more enlightened attitude to its 'sports' spread through society. Nonetheless, the squalid, tumble-down street remained until the widening of Farringdon Road and a programme of improvements to the Clerkenwell area in 1856–7 swept it away.

Holborn Restaurant

218 High Holborn was formerly a dance-hall, casino and swimming baths, but reopened in 1874 under Frederick Gordon as a spectacular public dining room. Among its diners was Gandhi, who ate here as a young law student in 1889 and found the setting quite palatial.

That same year the venue was extended and redecorated, and a decade later a Lieutenant-Colonel Newnham-Davies described eating there in his *Dinners and Diners*:

In the many-coloured marble hall, with its marble staircase springing from either side, a well-favoured gentleman with a close-clipped grey beard was standing, a sheet of paper in his hand, and waved us towards a marble portico, through which we passed to the grand saloon with its three galleries supported by marble pillars.

The restaurant offered a choice of locations to eat, including the Grand Salon, Duke's Salon, Ladies' Salon, Grill Room or Lincoln's Inn Buffet, as well as private dining rooms. Although clearly approving of the service and décor, Newnham-Davies was nonetheless somewhat scathing about the food: 'The cutlet of mutton that was brought to each of us was small, and had suffered from having to journey some way from the kitchen.'

An enduringly popular venue for reunions and annual suppers, the Holborn closed in 1955, in an asset sale prior to being demolished, it listed some 960 chairs for sale.

Holy Trinity

Minories, Tower Hill

FOUNDED IN 1108 BY MATILDA (Henry I's queen), from the late 13th century Holy Trinity served as a convent for an order known as the Poor Clares or Sister Minoresses (hence the street name, Minories).

It was granted papal exemption from the jurisdiction of the Archbishop of Canterbury and even after the dissolution of the monasteries, the church claimed the right to marry people without the calling of banns.

In the late 16th century, London's first great historian, John Stow, remembered as a child buying milk from the farm attached to the convent:

Near adjoining to this abbey, called the Minories, on the south side thereof, was some time a farm belonging to said nunnery; at the which farm I myself (in my youth) have fetched many a halfpenny worth of milk, and never had less than three ale-pints for a halfpenny in the summer, nor less than one ale-quart for a halfpenny in the winter, always hot from the cow, as the same was milked and strained.

Having escaped the Great Fire of 1666 unscathed, Holy Trinity fell into a state of dilapidation but was rebuilt in 1706. Sir Isaac Newton worshipped here when Master of the

Mint from 1699 to 1727. The church's tiny graveyard often overflowed with the dead and was emptied twice, in 1689 and 1763, though no one knows what happened to the bones. In 1852 a rather macabre discovery was made in the crypt when the head of Lady Jane Grey's father, the Duke of Suffolk, was found. Despite his having been beheaded on Tower Hill in 1554, his head remained well preserved and was displayed in a glass case by the pulpit for some time. Holy Trinity's long history only came to an end when it was destroyed by enemy bombing during the Second World War.

Horn Fair

Charlton

THIS FAIR, WHICH STARTED FROM CUCKOLD'S Point in Rotherhithe, was always a raucous and drunken affair, as might be expected of a celebration of illicit sexual relations.

Though disputed, the story of the fair's origins tells how King John, who reigned from 1199 to 1216, was hunting one day around Blackheath and Shooters Hill. Growing tired, he entered the house of a miller but no one was home except the miller's lovely young wife. Being a lusty young chap, John successfully set about wooing the lady but they were caught in flagrante by the returning miller.

Swearing to kill the interloper, the miller drew his dagger

and prepared to dispatch the unfortunate king, who was forced to reveal his identity to save his life. To placate the furious miller, John promised him all the land he could see on condition that he forgave his wife. Cuckold's Point marked the western limit of the miller's vision.

The people of the area were keen to tease their new overlord so held a celebration of the event on its anniversary, 18 October, the feast day of St Luke. They started their parade from Cuckold's Point, marked by a post bearing a pair of horns, and marched to Charlton village, where the real fun began.

The symbol of the horns had long been associated with those jealous and cheated in love, so the fair-goers all carried, wore or blew horns. Trinkets were sold (all made of horn, of course) and the fair became notorious for its drunken flirtations, with cross-dressing a far from unusual sight. In the early 18 century, Daniel Defoe described the goings-on at Charlton:

A village famous, or rather infamous for the yearly collected rabble of mad-people, at Horn-Fair; the rudeness of which I cannot but think, is such as ought to be suppressed, and indeed in a civiliz'd well govern'd nation, it may well be said to be unsufferable. The mob indeed at that time take all kinds of liberties, and the women are especially impudent for that day; as if it was a day that justify'd the giving themselves a loose to all manner of indecency and immodesty, without any reproach, or without suffering the censure which such behaviour would deserve at another time.

Completely at odds with Victorian mores, the fair was suppressed in 1874. A somewhat pale imitation of the original was reintroduced in the 1970s, providing a nice family day out rather than anything more ribald.

Islington Spa, or the New Tunbridge Wells

THIS WAS A CHALYBEATE SPRING (I.E. ONE containing much iron) that was discovered in 1683 by a Mr Sadler, surveyor of highways, in the grounds of the music hall he had just opened.

A pamphlet was written claiming that the waters were holy and had been famed for their healing powers until the knowledge of their properties was lost. Analysis conducted by the eminent scientist, Robert Boyle, showed the waters to be similar to the those at Tunbridge Wells.

The spa was soon attracting hypochondriacs from across the capital and by 1700 was quite the place to go. George Coleman gave his take on it in his 1776 farce, *The Spleen; or, Islington Spa*:

Gout hobbled there; Rheumatism groaned over his ferruginous water; severe coughs went arm-in-arm, chuckling as they hobbled; as for Hypochondria, he cracked jokes, he was in such high spirits at the thought of the new remedy.

In 1733 the Princesses Amelia and Caroline visited daily to drink the waters, and on their birthdays, as tradition dictated, they were saluted by 21 guns in Spa Fields as they passed. By now the business was attracting 1500 people daily, taking £30 per morning alone. A poem lauding the restorative qualities of the spring was hung in a local lodging house:

For three times ten years I travell'd the globe,
Consulted whole tribes of the physical robe;
Drank the waters of Tunbridge, Bath, Harrogate, Dulwich,
Spa, Epsom (and all by advice of the College);
But in vain, till to Islington waters I came,
To try if my cure would add to their fame.
In less than six weeks they produc'd a belief
This would be the place of my long-sought relief;
Before six weeks more had finished their course,
Full of spirits and strength, I mounted my horse,
Gave praise to my God, and rode cheerfully home,
Overjoy'd with the thoughts of sweet hours to come.
May Thou, great Jehovah give equal success
To all who resort to this place for redress!

To maximize his profits, Sadler put on entertainments – clowns, acrobats, musicians, dancers and the like – before future owners added new facilities in order to expand the scale of performances. The site has provided a home for the arts ever since and today you will find the Sadler's Wells Theatre here. As for the well, it was enshrined in a flint-and-seashell grotto around 1811 but by 1826 the coffee house constructed next to it had been demolished and the gardens were built over by 1840. The humble surrounding cottages were destroyed during the Second World War and the Spa Green Estate was built in their place, being completed in 1949.

Jacob's Island

Bermondsey

SOME YEARS AFTER THE INITIAL SERIALIZATION
of *Oliver Twist* in 1837, Dickens was attacked
over his portrayal of the site of Bill Sikes's death,
Jacob's Island.

Politicians refused to believe that such an awful place existed in their city. In a preface to a new edition of the book, Dickens wrote: 'In the year 1850 it was publicly declared by an amazed alderman that Jacob's Island did not exist and had never existed. Jacob's Island continues to exist (like an ill-bred place as it is) in the year 1867...'

Standing between the horribly polluted Neckinger River and a man-made ditch built as a mill-run for the medieval Bermondsey Abbey, Jacob's Island was a south London rookery similar in character to those at St Giles and Summertown. With a population of 7,286 people according to a survey of 1849, it was described in *The Morning Chronicle* thus:

On entering the precincts of the pest island, the air has literally the smell of a graveyard, and a feeling of nausea and heaviness comes over any one unaccustomed to imbibe the musty atmosphere. It is not only the nose, but the stomach, that tells how heavily the air is loaded with sulphuretted hydrogen; and as soon as you cross one of the crazy and rotting bridges over the reeking ditch, you know, as surely as if you had chemically tested

it, by the black colour of what was once the white-lead paint upon the door-posts and window-sills, that the air is thickly charged with this deadly gas. The inhabitants themselves show in their faces the poisonous influence of the mephitic air they breathe. Either their skins are white, like parchment, telling of the impaired digestion, the languid circulation, and the coldness of the skin peculiar to persons suffering from chronic poisoning, or else their cheeks are flushed hectically, and their eyes are glassy, showing the wasting fever and general decline of the bodily functions.

The ditches were filled in during the 1850s and many of the buildings were destroyed in a fire that raged for two weeks in 1861.

Jenny's Whim

Pimlico

A RED-BRICK AND LATTICE-WORK PUBLIC HOUSE
near Ebury Bridge, Pimlico, famed as the haunt
of lovers.

Named after either the original landlady and her fanciful gardens – replete with arbors and alcoves within which the amorous could exchange sweet nothings – or, alternatively, after a famous pyrotechnician from the reign of George 1, Jenny's Whim provided much the same as other pleasure gardens did but with a few added surprises. In *Henry Angelo's Reminiscences*, the author recorded that it was ... *much frequented from its novelty, being an inducement to allure the curious to it by its amusing deceptions. Here was a large garden; in different parts were recesses; and by treading on a spring – taking you by surprise – up started different figures, some ugly enough to frighten you outright – a harlequin, a Mother Shipton, or some terrific animal.*

Bowling, skittles and even duck-hunting were some of the other diversions available. Judging from an article in *The Connoisseur* of 15 May 1755, Jenny's Whim was particularly popular with the middle classes:

The lower sort of people have their Ranelaghs and their Vauxhalls ... Perrot's inimitable Grotto may be seen for only calling for a pot of beer; and the royal diversion of duck-hunting may be had into the bargain, together with a decanter of Dorchester, for your sixpence, at Jenny's Whim.

Some of the building survived until the 1860s but it was then demolished to make way for railway lines into Victoria Station.

Jonathan's Coffee House

Bank

OPENED IN 1680 BY JONATHAN MILES, THIS WAS the birth-place of the London Stock Exchange.

By 1690 there were over 100 companies trading their shares in the city and traders would meet at Jonathan's (and also at Garraway's Coffee House) to gather news from other traders and from merchants entering the city via the Thames. At Jonathan's, the news was written up on boards behind the bar.

Over time, traders developed a network of runners who would bring them all the latest on returning ships, whether it be tales of disaster and lost hauls or great successes. The runners would also elicit information from the servants of other merchants. When all this information was relayed back to the coffee shop, prices would rise or fall accordingly.

In 1689, John Castaing, an enterprising Huguenot broker, began writing a weekly list of stock and bullion prices and exchange rates, which he published on Tuesdays and Fridays as a sheet called *The Course of Exchange and Other Things.* Although there were other lists in circulation, Castaing's became

the premier source of financial information and was printed for the next hundred years.

When Jonathan's was burnt down in the Cornhill fire of 1748, it was immediately rebuilt with the support of various brokers and was given the name 'The Stock Exchange'. Jonathan's was also the venue for much of the speculative trading in the South Sea Company that led to the financially disastrous Bubble of 1720 which ruined the fortunes of many.

Kilburn Wells

'THIS HAPPY SPOT IS EQUALLY CELEBRATED FOR its rural situation, extensive prospects, and the acknowledged efficacy of its waters.'

So read the prospectus for Kilburn Wells and tea-rooms, published on 17 July 1773. Kilburn was an iron-rich chalybeate spring in the grounds of the long vanished Kilburn Abbey. Contained within the Bell Tavern, the spring was fitted with a pump in 1742 so that 'the politest of companies could come and drink the waters'.

Mildly purgative, milky in appearance and with a bitter taste, the water was said to contain more carbon dioxide than any other spring in Great Britain. It briefly rivalled Islington Spa in popularity and, 'being but a morning's walk from the metropolis', The Bell provided visitors with breakfast 'together with the best of wines and other liquors ... the great room being particularly adapted to the use and amusement ... fit for either music, dancing or entertainments'. The Bell was demolished in 1863; a stone plaque on Kilburn High Road and Belsize Road now marking the site.

King's Bench Prison

Borough

THIS PRISON STOOD ON THE SOUTH-WEST CORNER
of Blackman Street and Borough High Street
from the time of Richard II (1377–99).

Originally used to incarcerate those convicted at the travelling court of King's Bench, it became the debtors' prison for South London in the 1600s. In 1633 it held nearly 400 inmates with a collective debt of £900,000. Known for its cruelty, extortion, promiscuity and drunkenness, it was closed and moved to new premises in 1758.

The new prison, built in St George's Fields, Southwark, had 224 rooms (including eight state apartments) and a high surrounding wall. The regime there was considerably more relaxed, if one had the money to afford it. There were two pubs, a coffee house, thirty gins shops (selling 120 gallons of the spirit a week) and stalls offering meat, vegetables and pretty much anything else that might be wanted. It was described in 1828 as 'the most desirable place of incarceration in London'. Author Tobias Smollett wrote that the prison:

... appears like a neat little regular town, consisting of one street, surrounded by a very high wall, including an open piece of ground, which may be termed a garden, where the prisoners take the air, and amuse themselves with a variety of diversions. There are butchers' stands, chandlers' shops, a surgery, a tap-house, well frequented, and a public kitchen, in which provisions are dressed for all the prisoners gratis, at the expense of the publican.

A freedom of sorts could be purchased on a daily or yearly basis, on a promise to the governor not to travel outside of 'the rules' – a-three-mile area surrounding the prison. Income from 'the rules' in the early part of the 19th century was earning the governor £2823 each year, to say nothing of his slice of the beer sales – almost another £1000.

One of the prison's darkest days occurred when the radical MP John Wilkes was imprisoned here after his trial for seditious libel on 10 May 1768. His supporters massed at the gates, crying 'no justice, no peace'. Troops opened fire, killing seven and wounding fifteen in what became known as the St George's Fields Massacre. Imprisonment for debt was abolished in 1869 and afterwards King's Bench became a military prison until it was demolished in 1880.

King's Wardrobe

Blackfriars

**A 14TH-CENTURY HOUSE GIFTED TO EDWARD III
(1327–77) and used to hold all the ceremonial
clothes of the king, which had previously been
stored at the Tower of London.**

In addition, the Wardrobe contained all the clothes used by
the royal family for weddings and coronations, along with
state robes for ambassadors, the Prince of Wales, the Lord
Lieutenant of Ireland, the King's Ministers and Knights of
the Garter. It was a veritable museum of royal fashions over
a 400-year period.

The building was extended and eventually became so
large that it was restricting the income of St Andrew's-by-
the-Wardrobe, so 40 shillings (£2.00) was granted to the
rector of St Andrew's to cover the loss of tithes. When
the house was destroyed in the Great Fire of 1666, a new
location for the royal wardrobe was found on Buckingham
Street, although by the mid-17th century its significance
had declined. James I had allowed the Earl of Dunbar to sell
some of the contents and he 'sold, re-sold, and re-re-re-sold
... gaining vast estates thereby'.

The last 'Master of the Great Wardrobe' was appointed in
1775, but by then the role was merely a sinecure. Wardrobe
Place carries the memory of the building into the modern
era.

Kingsway Theatre

Holborn

**OPENING IN 1882 ON GREAT QUEEN STREET AS
the Novelty Theatre, this institution changed
hands and names with disconcerting frequency.**

In March 1883 it was known as the Folies-Dramatiques;
by 1888 it was the Jodrell; in 1889 it was once again the
Novelty; before being renamed as the New Queen's Theatre
in 1890; the Eden Palace of Theatre in 1894; the Great
Queen Street Theatre in 1907 and, later the same year, as
the Kingsway.

Intended as a comedy venue, it famously staged the
first English production of Ibsen's (largely laugh-free) *A
Doll's House*. A notorious event occurred in August 1896
during a performance of Frank Harvey's *Sins of the Night*,
when Wilfred Moritz Franks accidentally stabbed Temple E.
Crozier while on stage, with fatal consequences.

Having garnered something of a reputation for being
unlucky, the theatre was badly damaged on the night of
10/11 May 1941, the very last night of the Blitz. It never
reopened and was demolished in 1956. Much of the site
is now occupied by an office block and an extension of
Newton Street.

Leicester House

Leicester Square

BUILT IN THE 1630S IN WHAT WAS THEN KNOWN
as Leicester Fields, this was for a time one of the
biggest houses in London.

Grand though relatively plain on the outside, it had a
magnificent interior and was expensively furnished at the
behest of Robert Sidney, second Earl of Leicester.

The diarists Samuel Pepys and John Evelyn were both
entertained here, Pepys with the French Ambassador,
and Evelyn by Anne, Countess of Sunderland. One of the
entertainments that night was Richardson 'the famous fire-
eater, who before us devour'd brimstone on glowing coals,
chewing and swallowing them downe'.

After George, Prince of Wales, fought with his father, George I, at the baptismal font during the christening of his son, Frederick, the heir to the throne moved into Leicester House and ran a second court from here for ten years. Indeed, he was proclaimed king in front of its gate when the old king died. Later, the foppish and foolish Frederick would die in the house after being struck in the throat with a cricket ball in 1751.

The property subsequently came into the possession of the naturalist Aston Lever, who housed his vast accumulation of fossils within, and it opened to the public for fourteen years until it was moved to Blackfriars Rotunda in 1788. A keen archer, Lever formed the Toxophilite Society here in 1780.

Lillie Bridge Grounds

Earls Court

ON THE SITE OF WHAT IS NOW THE EARLS COURT
Exhibition Centre and a London Underground
maintenance depot, there once stood a
120,000-capacity sports stadium.

Opened in 1867, it was home to the Amateur Athletic Club, which was founded to organize the national athletics championships. A number of world records were set here, including a 4-min. 12¾-sec. mile by Goodall George in August 1886 (a mark that stood for twenty-eight years) and a high jump of 1.89 metres by Marshall Brooks in 1876.

The second ever FA Cup Final was held at the stadium in 1873, with Wanderers beating Oxford University 2-0. The event, though, was badly attended, attracting a crowd of only 3,000 as it clashed with the Oxford vs Cambridge boat race. The Middlesex County Cricket Club was also based at the ground until 1872 but left because of the poor quality of the turf. Other sports hosted here included wrestling, cycling and boxing, including the very first amateur bouts with prizes presented by John Douglas, the Marquis of Queensberry (author of the sport's defining Queensberry Rules and bête noire of Oscar Wilde).

Though famed for its support of amateur sports, the stadium came to a sad end as a result of professionalism. A sprint race between Harry Gent and Harry Hutchens in 1887 had attracted large-scale betting but when the runners' promoters failed to agree on who should lose, the race was cancelled and the crowd rioted, burning down the grandstand. Falling into ruins, it was closed in 1888.

Lincoln's Inn Fields Theatre

**OPENED ON PORTUGAL STREET IN 1660 BY
Sir William d'Avenant.**

This was the first modern theatre in England with both a proscenium arch and moveable scenery. Samuel Pepys recounted a visit on 20 November 1660:

Mr Shepley and I to the new play-house near Lincoln's Inn

Fields, which was formerly Gibbon's Tennis Court. ... Here I saw for the first time one Moone [Michael Mohun, 1616?–84], who is said to be the best actor in the world, lately come over with the king; and, indeed, it is the finest play-house, I believe, that ever was in England.

Thomas Betterton, one of the great actors of the age, made his debut here in *Hamlet*. Pepys was present again, noting: 'Betterton did the Prince's part beyond all imagining.'

Having sworn off plays in favour of hard work and advancement, Pepys was in the locale again in May 1667 and, seeing Charles II's mistress there, was sorely tempted to break his vows: '... but Lord! how it went against my heart to go away from the very door of the Duke's play-house, and my Lady Castlemayne's coach, and many great coaches there, to see *"The Siege of Rhodes"*.'

By then under the management of Betterton, the Duke's Company moved out of the theatre in 1674 and the building was once again used as tennis courts until Betterton led a return in 1695. After a ten-year stint, the Company moved on once more in 1705 and the theatre fell into disrepair until it was taken over by Christopher Rich, a lawyer, and his son John Rich, a talented dancer. Having renovated the building and installed seating for 1400, the Riches staged John Gay's *The Beggar's Opera*, the most successful play of the century. Based loosely on the lives of Jack Sheppard and Jonathan Wilde, it was the production that was said to have made 'Gay rich and Rich gay'. The last performances at the theatre were in 1744 and afterwards it was used as an auction house before being demolished to make way for an extension to the Royal College of Surgeons.

London Bridge

Some notable decapitated heads
displayed thereon

LONDON BRIDGE HAS LONG BEEN CENTRAL TO LIFE
in the capital but one of its more macabre purposes
was as a site for the display of traitors' heads,
impaled upon spikes to serve as a warning to others.

In the late 16th century, Paul Hentzner, a German visitor to
the city, made some notes on the bridge: 'Upon this is built a
tower, on whose top the heads of such as have been executed
for high treason are placed on iron spikes: we counted above
thirty.' Here is a roll call of a few of the unfortunates from
throughout the centuries.

1305   William Wallace (Scottish rebel)

1306   Sir Simon Fraser (Scottish rebel)
1407   Henry Percy, Earl of Northumberland
1408   Lord Bardolf
1431   A rebel weaver from Abingdon
1450   Jack Cade and nine of his captains (Kentish rebels)
1496   Flamock and Joseph (Cornish rebels)
1500s   Several Lollards
1535   John Fisher, Bishop of Rochester
1535   Sir Thomas More, former Lord Chancellor
1540   Thomas Cromwell, Earl of Essex
1605   Father Garnet (Gunpowder Plot conspirator)

London Bridge Waterworks

THE MANY PILLARS SUPPORTING LONDON BRIDGE
caused the waters of the Thames to flow at great
speeds. A German engineer, Pieter Morice, thus
proposed that a waterwheel be placed in one of
the arches to pump water around the city, having
seen similar schemes work in his native land.

Granted a lease for 500 years at 10 shillings (50p) per annum,
he built his first waterwheel in 1581 and began pumping water
supplies to the city on Christmas Eve of 1582. The success of the
scheme enabled him to lease another arch shortly afterwards so
that by the time of the Great Fire in 1666, Morice's descendants
were generating an income of over £1000 a year from the
business he started.

However, the enterprise fared badly in the conflagration and had to be rebuilt, reopening for business in 1669. The Morices sold their stake in 1701 and by 1737 a fourth wheel had been added to those already operating. Together they pumped over 100,000 gallons per hour, with supplies to the south of the city aided by the presence of another wheel at Southwark.

By 1821 it is estimated that 4 million gallons of water were being supplied daily. Although its quality was admittedly foul, if allowed to stand for twenty-four hours it was adjudged to be 'finer than any other water that could be produced'. However, when the bridge was rebuilt in 1822, its new design precluded the use of waterwheels and responsibility for the city's water supplies was transferred to the New River Company.

London Salvage Corps

By 1866 it had become clear to the city's major insurers that the cost of fire damage could be reduced if goods and furniture (along with any inhabitants, of course) could be more efficiently rescued from burning buildings.

Therefore, eighteen companies, including Lloyd's of London, banded together to form the London Salvage Corps.

Working alongside the Fire Brigade, its personnel attempted to salvage property before it became too seriously damaged by water or smoke. Made up mainly of members recruited from the Royal Navy, it was based in Watling Street and used horse-drawn carriages until 1923, when a variety of red motor tenders were added. When the Corps was disbanded in 1984, its duties were taken over by the London Fire Brigade.

Lowther Arcade

The Strand

ONCE ONE OF THE MOST FAMOUS SIGHTS IN London, this was a 210ft glass-covered shopping arcade known especially for its toy shops.

Built after the 1830 improvement works on the Strand, it was the delight of countless Victorian children.

In the arcade's northern part was the Adelaide Gallery, also know as the 'National Gallery of Practical Science, Blending Instruction with Amusement'. *In Sketches of London Life and Character* (1849), Albert Smith gave an account of it:

Clever professors were there, teaching elaborate sciences in lectures of twenty minutes each; fearful engines revolved, and hissed, and quivered, as the fettered steam that formed their entrails grumbled sullenly in its bondage; mice led gasping subaqueous lives in diving-bells; clock-work steamers ticked round and round a basin perpetually, to prove the efficacy of invisible paddles; and on all sides were clever machines which stray visitors were puzzled to class either as coffee-mills, water-wheels, roasting-jacks, or musical instruments. There were artful

snares laid for giving galvanic shocks to the unwary; steam-guns that turned bullets into bad sixpences against the target; and dark microscopic rooms for shaking the principles of teetotalers, by showing the wriggling abominations in a drop of the water which they were supposed daily to gulp down.

In 1840 the hall was an amusement arcade and by 1852 the Adelaide Gallery was housing the Royal Marionette Theatre. Lowther Arcade itself was demolished in 1904, with Coutts Bank building new premises on the site.

Lyons Corner Houses

WITH THEIR DISTINCTIVE GOLD-AND-WHITE
shop fronts, this was one of the best-known restaurant
chains not only in London but around the country.

Lyons opened its first teashop at 213 Piccadilly in 1894. However, it was with their massive eateries that they really captured the public's imagination.

The Coventry Street Corner House, for instance, was opened in 1909 and had seating for 4500 customers over five floors. Two other restaurants, on Tottenham Court Road and the Strand, could each feed 2500. The company kept prices down by catering on a vast scale, with the Corner Houses offering different menus on different floors, along with bespoke musical accompaniment. Indeed, by 1930 Lyons was employing so many musicians that it had its own Orchestral Department. Meanwhile, 'Nippies' – the name given to female serving staff – passed into the popular lexicon, with the name even registered by the company in 1924.

Founded by Messers Gluckstein, Salmon and Lyons, Lyons teashops spread firstly across London, and then throughout the nation until there were 250 sites. J Lyons and Co Ltd also catered for corporate clients, including Buckingham Palace, the Wimbledon Lawn Tennis Association and the Chelsea Flower Show. By 1887 it was the biggest food-manufacturing company in Europe. However, come the 1970s the company had overreached itself financially and was dismantled and sold off, the last Corner House closing its doors in 1977.

Molly Houses

LITTLE IS KNOWN ABOUT THE FULL HISTORY OF
Molly Houses, as they were secretive places where
homosexuals could meet and enjoy each other's
company, without the risk of prosecution.

The Buggery Act of 1533 made sodomy a crime punishable by
either a fine, the pillory and even death. Old Bailey records from
1726 provide us a small insight into one of the capital's most
famous – Mother Clap's, on Field Lane, Holborn. Following
the execution for sodomy of Gabriel Lawrence, William Griffin
and George Kedear in May 1726, Margaret Clap was herself
brought before the judges, charged with keeping a house
in which 'she procur'd and encourag'd Persons to commit
Sodomy'.

One Samuel Stevens gave the evidence: *I found near Men
Fifty there, making Love to one another as they call'd it. Sometimes
they'd sit in one anothers Laps, use their Hands indecently Dance
and make Curtsies and mimick the Language of Women – O Sir!
– Pray Sir! – Dear Sir! Lord how can ye serve me so! – Ah ye little
dear Toad! Then they'd go by Couples, into a Room on the same
Floor to be marry'd as they call'd it. They talk'd all manner of the
most vile Obscenity in her Presence, and she appear'd wonderfully
pleas'd with it.*

Margaret was found guilty and sentenced to the pillory. It
is thought that she died of the injuries she received there. It is
sometime assumed that Margaret Clap gave her name to Molly
Houses – Molly being a popular shortening of Margaret, but
the activities of two of the city's most fearsome crime bosses a

decade earlier would suggest otherwise.

Before bearing the self proclaimed title of 'Thief Taker General of England and Ireland' Jonathan Wild, a failed button maker from Wolverhampton, had been trying to steal the business off his predecessor, one Christopher Hitchin. In 1718 Hitchin published a broadside – a one sheet pamphlet – called *A Trout the City of London.* This was an attempt to expose Wild for what he really was, a underworld crime boss and receiver of stolen goods, (as was Hitchins himself). The tactic disastrously backfired when Wild countered with *An answer to a Late Insolent Libel,* the main thrust being that Hitchin frequented Molly Houses and enjoyed the pleasures thereof.

With Hitchin's reputation destroyed, Wild went on to enjoy unprecedented power, posing as a saviour for the capital's crime problem, whilst at the same time running a network of criminals, and even chartering vessels to transport his ill-gotten gains abroad to Holland, where they could be sold. Thankfully he was found out and executed at Tyburn on 24 May 1725.

Mudlarks

OF ALL THE DESPERATE JOBS THAT THE LONDON poor pursued in order to eke out a living, among the most depressing was that of the mudlark.

When the capital was still a thriving port city unloading goods from around the globe, the shoreline of the Thames was a workplace for these pathetic creatures.

Nearly always young children whose terrible family circumstances had forced them into a truly pitiable state, mudlarks collected goods such as coal, old rope, nails and cloth that had fallen from vessels docked in the Pool of London – the area immediately downstream of London Bridge. Henry Mayhew, in his *London Labour and the London Poor* (1851), recounted an interview with one of the sorry orphans, describing him thus:

He was fourteen years old. He had two sisters, one fifteen and the other twelve years old. His father had been dead for 9 years … He had fallen (in a state of intoxifaction) between two barges … He [the boy] went into the river, up to his knees, and in searching for the mud often ran pieces of glass and long nails into his feet. Having dressed his wound he would immediately return to the river-side directly.

Mayhew estimated that almost 300 children made a living in this way.

Necropolis Railway

Waterloo

MASSIVE URBAN EXPANSION DURING THE 1800S had led to horrendous over-crowding in the city's 200 burial sites.

This crisis resulted in mass graves, bodies spilling out of the ground, and outbreaks of cholera and typhus. Indeed, so dire was the situation that the government passed the Burial

Act of 1851, banning all interments in built-up areas.

To cope with the huge numbers of burials, Brookwood Cemetery in Surrey was opened in November 1854. At the time it was the largest graveyard in the world, and was connected to London by the Necropolis Railway, which originally ran from a separate platform at Waterloo Station. Waterloo was chosen for its proximity to the Thames and the ease of transporting bodies along the river.

With its entrance on Westminster Bridge Road, the Necropolis Railway had a variety of waiting rooms for different mourning parties and catered for 1st-, 2nd- and 3rd-class funerals. A steam lift raised coffins to the private platform on the first floor. Frederick Engels, one of the fathers of modern communism, made his final journey from the station on 10 August 1895, before being cremated and his ashes scattered at Beachy Head.

Increased use of Waterloo Station by living commuters led to a new station for the dead being built on the west side of Westminster Bridge Road. It opened in 1902, its entrance still visible at No 188, although the word 'Necropolis' has been covered up. The station was bombed during the final stages of the Blitz in April 1941 and by the end of hostilities it was considered economically unviable to re-open the station or the route to Brookwood.

When the line had first opened, it had been expected that 50,000 of the city's dead would travel along its tracks each year. After 90 years of service, in fact only just over 200,000 had boarded its trains, the first being a pair of stillborn twins from Borough on 13 November 1854 and the last a Chelsea Pensioner, Edward Irish, who was born in 1868 and died on 11 April 1941.

Newgate Prison

Old Bailey

BUILT ON THE SITE OF TODAY'S OLD BAILEY,
Newgate was the city's principal prison from at
far back as the 12th century. Over its long history,
it inhabited a variety of buildings that variously
fell into ruin or were burnt down by rioters.

The jail was originally housed in the Newgate, the fifth of
London's gates built during the reign of Stephen or Henry I. In
1423, Richard Whittington, he of the famous cat and three
times the capital's mayor, left money in his will for the 're-
edification of Newgate Prison' but by then it was in one of its
periods of ruin. Having subsequently been rebuilt, it burnt
down in the Great Fire of London, only to be rebuilt again by

1672 with 'great magnificence' externally, though conditions for the inmates inside were as appalling as ever.

Described as a 'prototype for hell' by Henry Fielding, it suffered from a poor water supply, virtually non-existent ventilation and repellant odours. Outbreaks of disease, known as 'jail fever', were common. One outbreak in the 1700s swept through the prison and into the neighbouring Old Bailey, to which it was connected by a walkway, killing not only convicts but also judges, barristers and jurors. In total, sixty court officials died, prompting some attempts to improve the air by building a ventilation tower. Two workers died of noxious inhalations during construction, while neighbouring residents complained that they too were now being poisoned, while very little difference was felt in the conditions inside.

If the sanitation was terrible, then the jail regime to which prisoners were subjected can only be described as fiendish. New arrivals were clapped in irons, the weight of them dependent on how much they could pay the keeper. In general, wealth bought privileges, from beds and bedding to rooms higher up in the building, further away from the stench, filth and misery that constituted daily life on the lower floors.

The poorest convicts could expect to be housed in the Stone Hold, which one inmate of the 1720s described as; 'a terrible stinking dark and dismal place situated underground into which no daylight can come. It was paved with stone, the prisoners had no beds and lay on the pavement.' Prisoners were expected to provide and cook their own food, even having to pay for the privilege of sitting closer to the fire. For those who could afford it, drink was freely available but it is difficult to imagine the squalid misery that made up most inmates' lives.

The majority of London's most famous (and infamous) criminals passed through Newgate's doors, either to be released, transported or executed. Among them were Titus Oates (who fabricated evidence of a popish plot against the crown), Jonathan Wild (the Thief-Taker General) and the writer Daniel Defoe. Stories of daring escapes are plentiful and success usually relied on either bribery or daring-do. None was more extraordinary than that of Jack Sheppard, a house-breaker and former carpenter whose escape from the Castle (a room high in one of the towers) made him a working-class hero.

Sheppard was kept chained to the floor, manacled and handcuffed, but on Saturday, 10 October 1724, he managed to break his bonds, climb up the inside of a chimney, break through seven doors (one of which hadn't been opened for fourteen years) and scramble on to the roof. He was about to jump down to freedom when he lost his nerve as he considered the great height. With unbelievable and brazen audacity, the prisoner returned to his cell to fetch a blanket, made his way back to the roof and used the blanket to lower himself to a nearby house, from where he made good his escape. When he was eventually recaptured and returned to captivity, he was visited by the great and good of the day, many of whom appealed (unsuccessfully) for clemency on his behalf. Sheppard met his death at Tyburn on Monday, 16 November 1724, in front of a vast crowd of 200,000 people and went on to be immortalized in ballads, plays and even a famous novel.

A new prison was built from 1770 to 1778 on the designs of George Dance the Younger, a reincarnation described as 'very large, beautiful and strong' but destined not to last long. On the night of 5 June 1780, riots inspired by the anti-Catholic rabble-rousing of Lord George Gordon led to the prison being stormed, its inmates being released and its buildings burnt down. The new Newgate, completed in 1783, admitted Lord Gordon himself, who died there in 1793 of jail fever. When Tyburn was no longer used for public hangings, the spectacle continued outside Newgate until 1868, after which time hangings were conducted inside the prison. The jail was finally demolished in 1902.

New River Head

Clerkenwell

THE PROBLEMS ASSOCIATED WITH HOW BEST to supply fresh water to the capital had been a matter of concern from as early as the 13th century.

Then a scheme began bringing water from Tyburn in 3000 yards of lead piping to a conduit at Cheapside. However, by the late Elizabethan period the situation had reached crisis point and it was suggested that a stream from Hertfordshire, or thereabouts, should be diverted.

Two Acts of Parliament were passed to allow the project to go ahead but it wasn't until King James 1's jeweller, Hugh Myddleton, took charge of affairs that work started in earnest. Digging of a channel from Amwell and Chadwell in Hertforshire was finished in 1613 and the 38-mile cutting was officially opened on 29 September that year. The project had only been possible thanks to a secret cash injection from

James I, who remained a sleeping partner.

The path of the New River became a popular destination for holidaying Londoners over the next 200 years and proved a delight for anglers and lovers alike. The water's slow flow meant that it was prone to the 'development of lower forms of animal and vegetable life', so filtration beds were opened in Stoke Newington in 1852. However, the watercourse gradually became covered over and built upon so that by 1900 it had all but disappeared from view above ground. Direct flow to New River Head ended in 1946 and today the river ends in Stoke Newington.

New River House, the former headquarters of the Metropolitan Water Board, now marks the spot where fresh water once flowed. The surrounding streets bear testimony to its history; River Street, Amwell Street and Myddleton Square. The pub on Amwell Street was named The Fountain, though in recent years it has sadly been rebranded.

Nine Elms Railway Station

**ONE OF THE MANY LOST STATIONS OF LONDON,
Nine Elms was the original – though short-lived
– terminus for the London and South Western
Railway, which opened on 21 May 1838.**

Its greatest moment came nine days after it opened, when newspapers advertised special trains to the Epsom Derby and 5000 passengers turned up to catch them.

However, the station was inconveniently situated away from other central transport hubs and struggled for popularity. It was closed to passengers in 1848 when Waterloo Bridge Station (the 'Bridge' was subsequently dropped) opened. Nine Elms, meanwhile, was converted to a shunting and goods yard. It was bombed in 1941 and demolished in the 1960s, with the flower section of New Covent Garden Market now standing where it used to be.

Nonsuch House

London Bridge

THIS WAS POSSIBLY THE WORLD'S FIRST prefabricated building, having been designed and manufactured in Holland.

The four-storey wooden structure was shipped to London and erected on London Bridge, quickly becoming one of the best-known sights in the city. The name Nonsuch is a clear allusion to its unique status – no such other being known of – and may also have been a reference to Henry VIII's palace built on the outskirts of London in 1538.

Completed in 1578, Nonsuch House stood over the edifice's seventh and eighth arches from the Southwark side, completely straddling the bridge. No nails were used in its construction but wooden pegs held the structure together instead. With elaborate Dutch stepped gables that overhung both sides of the bridge, the building was covered in ornate carved decorations and had square towers at each corner sporting onion domes, making it visible from all over the city. A sundial on the house's south side bore the legend: 'Time and tide stay for no man.'

Old Clothes Exchange

Houndsditch

FOR MANY YEARS THE RAG FAIR, AT WHICH SECOND-hand clothing was bought and sold, was held in the environs of Petticoat Lane. So frantic could trading become that the market gained a reputation for rowdiness, with brawls a commonplace sight.

In *London Labour and the London Poor*, Henry Mayhew demonstrates typical prejudices of the time by blaming the Irish, who made up a large proportion of the buyers, and the Jews, who he said controlled the trade. He wrote: 'The passion of the Irish often drove them to resort to cuffs, kicks and blows, which the Jews, although with a better command over their tempers, were not slack in returning.' Often upwards of 200 police constables were needed to keep the peace.

The trade was eventually regularized by the opening of the Old Clothes Exchange in Phil's Building, Houndsditch, in 1843. Most of the garments were sold by weight to traders from Dublin, although there were dealers from as far afield as Scotland, Holland and Belgium, as well as other English cities. A small charge was levied on anyone who entered the Exchange and was collected by former prize fighters who acted as bouncers. The brisk trade generated a turnover of some £1500 a week.

Old Slaughter's Coffee House

Covent Garden

ONE OF THE MOST FAMOUS GEORGIAN COFFEE houses, Old Slaughter's, opened at Nos 74–75 St Martin's Lane in 1692. It was named after its original proprietor, Thomas Slaughter, who died in 1740.

Like other coffee houses of the era, it attracted a particular clientele, which in this case was an artistic crowd who wished to talk and discuss business without the distractions of the tavern. The exclusion of women meant that, unlike the pubs of the day, gentlemen could chat without being bothered by prostitutes, or, as suited the more misogynistic visitor, women in general. Earnest discussion was the order of the day, with the Irish writer, Oliver Goldsmith, noting: 'If a man be passionate he may vent his rage among the old orators at Slaughter's Chop house and damn the nation because it keeps him from starving.'

Many artists and artisans who lived and worked in

Covent Garden used the premises as an office, often receiving mail here, some of which correspondence makes it possible to draw up an impressive list of some of Old Slaughter's many talented visitors. William Hogarth and Thomas Gainsborough were both regulars, as were the painters William Kent, Thomas Hudson and Francis Hayman, the engraver Hubert Gravelot, the sculptor Francois Roubilliac, medalist Richard Yeo, and the architects James Payne, Robert Adam and Isaac Ware.

Slaughter's also hosted the first ever meeting of the Royal Society for the Prevention of Cruelty to Animals in 1824 but the building was demolished in 1843 to make way for the construction of Cranbourn Street.

Pantheon

Oxford Street

**OPENING TO GREAT FANFARE IN 1772, THE
Pantheon was one of the largest rooms in England.**

Designed by James Wyatt, it was intended that its entertainments should attract some of the crowd from Ranelagh Gardens, the pleasure gardens located in Chelsea, come the winter season. A city guide of the time described how its 'interior, in point of extent, design, convenience of arrangement, and beauty of execution united' was 'unequalled by anything of the kind in London, or even in Europe'. The building was topped with a domed roof roughly based on Santa Sophia in Istanbul.

Here the great and good were invited to masquerades, fetes and concerts, with the opportunity to visit card rooms, drink tea or have supper in between the entertainments. Horace Walpole gave the Pantheon a most enthuasiastic review:

It amazed me myself. Imagine Balbec in all its glory! The pillars are of artificial giallo antico. The ceilings, even of the passages, are of the most beautiful stuccos in the best taste of grotesque. The ceilings of the ball-rooms and the panels are painted like Raphael's loggias in the Vatican. A dome like the Pantheon, glazed.

Nonetheless, its popularity soon declined and in 1791 it was converted into a theatre. A disastrous fire in January 1792 completely gutted the building but, following a rebuild by Chrispus Clagett, it re-opened in 1795. It was not a success, though, and Clagett soon disappeared, leaving huge debts. The massive cost of upkeep continually hampered new ventures. Neither the efforts of the National Institute for Improving Manufacturing nor the expansion of Henry Greville's Argyll Rooms were able to make it profitable, and in 1813 it once again reverted to serving as a theatre.

Alas, the promoter Nicholas Cundy attempted to stage plays here despite being unlicensed to do so, so the Pantheon was closed by order of the Lord Chamberlain. Meanwhile, its interior was stripped of its fixtures and fittings. It was subsequently converted into a bazaar and then, in 1867, a wine warehouse. The premises were sold to Marks & Spencer in 1937, who demolished what remained of the original building and erected the store that sits on Oxford Street today.

Paris Gardens

Bankside

THIS WAS THE SITE OF LONDON'S FIRST PLEASURE gardens, although from our modern perspective 'pleasure' might seem a dubious label.

Here originally stood the manor house of Robert De Paris and later the home of Jane Seymour, Henry VIII's third wife. Its gardens had opened to the public and were being marked on maps as early as 1574. The site extended from the current Southwark Bridge to the western side of Blackfriars Bridge, its approximate area still measurable by the streets that continue to bear the names of Bear Gardens and Paris Gardens. Southwark had long been a favourite haunt of pleasure-seeking city-dwellers, lying as it did outside the jurisdiction of the city elders.

Bear-baiting was a popular spectacle here, along with dog- and cock-fights, as well as prize fighting. But visitors could pursue almost any leisure activity (illicit or not) that they might choose, from theatrical performances (both the Globe and the Rose theatres were built in Paris Gardens) to rendezvous with local prostitutes (or Winchester Geese as they were known, so called because they were licensed by the Bishop of Winchester).

The Gardens' bear pits were built in the style of amphitheatres, with banked wooden seating that on several occasions collapsed, resulting in the deaths of several spectators. One such notable incident occurred one Sunday in 1582, which

Puritan elders celebrated as being 'heaven-directed'. Yet even these tragedies did not seem to dampen Londoners' ardour for the sport, and for many years the Gardens were under royal patronage. Elizabeth I, for instance, was said to be a keen fan of bear-baiting and visited several times.

The theatre impresario Edward Alleyn (1566–1626) was for some time the 'keeper of the king's beasts or 'master of the royal bear gardens' and derived an annual income of £500 from the position, which goes some way to illustrating the popularity of animal contests during this time. Alleyn went on to found Dulwich College and many other philanthropic enterprises, all of which have something to thank animal-baiting for.

Although bear-baiting was suppressed during the period of the Commonwealth (1653-1659), the Gardens re-emerged with the restoration of Charles II in 1660. Diarist Samuel Pepys recorded a visit to watch a prize fight here on 28 May 1667:

Abroad, and stopped at Bear-garden Stairs, there to see a prize fought. But the house so full there was no getting in there, so forced to go through an ale-house into the pit, where the bears are baited; and upon a stool did see them fight, which they did very furiously, a butcher and a waterman. The former had the better all along, till by-and-by the latter dropped his sword out of his hand, and the butcher, whether or not seeing his sword dropped I know not, but did give him a cut over the wrist, so as he was disabled to fight any longer. But Lord! to see in a minute how the whole stage was full of watermen to revenge the foul play, and the butchers to defend their fellow, though most blamed him: and there they all fell to it, knocking and cutting down many on each side. It was pleasant to see; but that I stood in the pit and feared that in the tumult I might get some hurt. At last the battle broke up, and so I away.

Perhaps unsurprisingly, Paris Gardens won for itself a shady reputation. Being unlit at night, it was reputedly a hangout for conspirators, with one 17th-century commentator noting: 'This may better bee termed a foule dene than a faire garden … here come few that either regard their credit or losse of time: the swaggering Roarer, the cunning Cheater, the rotten Bawd and the bloudy Butcher all have their rendezvous here.'

Much of the Gardens was developed during the 17th century, while the popularity of bear-baiting went into decline until it was eventually banned in 1835. The last recorded incidence of animal-baiting at Paris Gardens recorded on 2 April 1682.

Patterers, or Death Hunters

LONDON'S UNDERCLASS ALWAYS STRUGGLED TO earn a living and forever sought inventive ways to make a penny or two.

The 1800s saw the emergence of patterers – men who gathered intelligence on the streets to reproduce in newspapers, pamphlets and tracts which they sold on the public highway. They typically lured potential customers by describing recent murders or reporting the last words of the condemned to passers-by, hence their alternative name, 'Death Hunters'.

Titles such as *The Life of Calcraft, the Hangman and The Diabolical Practises of Dr, ---- on his patients when in a state of mesmorism* were their stock in trade. They also did good business in 'secret packages', which would either contain pornographic material or, as some of the unwary found to their cost, nothing at all.

In making his exhaustive study of the capital's underclass, Henry Mayhew discovered that patterers were exclusively male and had a cant, or slang, all of their own that was in some ways a forerunner of Cockney rhyming slang:

Crabshells	*shoes*	Balmy	*insane*
Kite	*paper*	Mill tag	*a shirt*
Nests	*varieties*	Smeesh	*a shift*
Sticky	*wax*	Hay-bay	*a woman*
Toff	*gentlemen*	Doxy	*a wife*
Burerk	*lady*	Flam	*a lie*
Camister	*minister*	Teviss	*a shilling*
Crocus	*doctor*	Bull	*a crown*

Penny Gaffs

While the 19th-century upper and middle classes could frequent London's multitude of regularized theatres, the poor were excluded from them by the entrance fee alone.

They weren't, however, without theatres that played to their tastes. Shop-front theatres, called Penny Gaffs, sprang up in the poorer parts of town, hosting up to six shows an evening. A penny was charged for admission and shows typically consisted of a musical performance, lewd dancing and a 'vulgar' comic. A Victorian visitor reported his trip to one of the least offensive shows he could find 'in the environs of Smithfield': 'The visitors were all boys and girls. They stood laughing and joking with the lads, in an unconcerned, impudent manner that was most appalling.' The shop in question had had its first floor removed to make a larger space, and an audience of about 200 people was present. 'One woman carrying a sickly child with a bulging forehead, was reeling drunk with saliva running down her mouth as she stared about her with a heavy fixed eye,' reported the appalled guest.

An 8ft stage contained not only the performers but also a piano and space for a violinist. The one-hour performance consisted mainly of singing and dancing, including a comic singer who was greeted with rapturous applause and who sang a song: *the whole point of which consisted of the utterance of some filthy words at the end of each stanza ... In this, not a single chance had been missed: ingenuity had been exerted to its utmost lest an obscene thought should be passed by, and it was absolutely awful to behold the relish with which the young ones jumped to the meaning of the verses.*

That was not the end of the night's entertainment, either. There followed a ballet dance between a man and a woman that shocked our audience member to his very boots:

If there had been any feat of agility, any grimacing, or, in fact, anything with which the laughter of the uneducated classes is usually associated, the applause might be accounted for: but here were two ruffians degrading themselves each time they stirred a limb, and forcing the brains of the childish audience before them to thoughts that embitter a lifetime.

Peerless Pool

Shoreditch

**THE PRECURSOR TO ALL LONDON'S LIDOS (OR
open-air swimming pools) was the subject of a
wonderful piece of rebranding. Located on Old
Street, this was an ancient spring famed in the
17th century for its duck-hunting but with a
reputation for accidents.**

The London historian, John Stow, once called it Perilous
Pond due to the number of young men who had drowned
in it. In 1752 it was converted at considerable expense into
a gravel-bottomed swimming pool by the jeweller William
Kemp, opening in its new guise as the Peerless Pool in 1752.

It measured 170 x 108ft and was filled with water to a
maximum depth of 5 feet. Kemp charged an entry fee of one
shilling, making it the preserve of the wealthy, who had access
to marble changing rooms. Shaded by fine trees, the pool
soon became a popular city resort. For a hundred years people
came to swim in the summer and skate in the winter but by
1850 it had been built over. The nearby Peerless Street and
Bath Street are now the only indicators that it was ever here.

Swimming, however, went on to take the capital by storm,
and the 1930s saw an explosion in the growth of lidos, almost
all of which have now been lost to redevelopment.

Pillory

✦

IN THE PAST, dairymen 'selling mingled butter' were 'sharply corrected' upon the pillory.

So also were 'fraudulent corn, coal, and cattle dealers, cutters of purses, sellers of sham gold rings, keepers of infamous houses, forgers of letters, bonds, and deeds, counterfeits of papal bulls, users of unstamped measures, and forestallers of the markets'.

The medieval punishment of standing in the pillory saw the culprit strapped into a wooden contraption that held the hands and head exposed as the good folk of the town hurled abuse, rotten fruit and often much, much worse at the offender. The principal locations of London's pillories were Cheapside, Cornhill, Old Bailey, Palace Yard and Charing Cross. Other temporary pillories were regularly erected elsewhere, including Clerkenwell Green and St James's.

Should a magistrate have considered a particular crime worthy of extra punishment, additional grotesque forms of retribution could be added to the sentence. For instance, those found guilty of spreading rumours might have their ears nailed to the pillory. William Prynne, a lawyer and vociferous opponent of the established church, was pilloried three times in the 1630s. He had one ear cut off while pilloried at Palace Yard, and the second was removed at Cheapside. Imprisoned for life, he continued to write seditious tracts and was pilloried again, and the letters S and L (for 'Seditious Libeler') branded on his cheeks.

Many lost their lives in the pillory, the reaction of the public being so vehement against them. Others fared better though, such as Daniel Defoe who claimed he was pelted with flowers when he was given a sentence for attacking unpopular practices in the church. The punishment was formally abolished in 1837, James Peter Bossy having the dubious honour of being the last man to endure it on 24 June 1830 at the Old Bailey.

Plague Pits

CONSIDERING THAT THEY SO FILL THE imagination, evidence of plague pits – large mass graves built outside the populated areas of the city to accommodate mass deaths – are very scant indeed.

Mass graves were undoubtedly dug, but the vast majority of these were in traditional graveyards. The records of St Bride's Church for the period of the last great outbreak of plague, in 1665, show that although a vast number of parishioners died – over 2000 – they were nearly all accommodated in one of the church's three graveyards.

Daniel Defoe in his *Journal of the Plague Year* records having seen new mass graves being dug in a variety of city churchyards, although how much veracity we can place on his information is debatable. His book, which is more novel than reportage, was written in 1722. Defoe was 4, or possibly 6 years old at the time of the plague, his date of birth being unsure.

At various times large numbers of bones have been discovered when new Tube lines are dug, or when new buildings erected. The Broadgate construction around Liverpool Street Station uncovered a vast quantity – but these are thought to have been the dead from the original Bedlam Hospital which once occupied the area.

Samuel Pepys makes no mention of plague pits in his diary for 1665 – and he lived and stayed in the city for much of the time. It is likely, though, that Bunhill Fields was first opened to bury the plague dead at the height of the infestation in August 1665.

The most enduring myth is that Blackheath is so named as it was the burial site used during the Black Death (1348-1350), although this is untrue. Recorded in 1166 , nearly 200 years beforehand as 'Blachehedfeld' – it is derived from the colour of the soil – black.

Pure Collectors

**The expansion of industry in the capital
demanded that raw materials be imported from
all over the world.**

But the tanning businesses of Bermondsey – remembered in road names such as Leather Lane and Leathermarket Street – needed one particular resource that the capital's working class could collect for themselves on the very streets where they walked: dog dung.

Called 'pure' because of its cleansing property when curing leather, it was gathered by the bucketful. The white variety was the most valuable so collectors were often found to have adulterated their finds with mortar from walls. It is estimated that when the tanning industry was at its peak, 300 people made a living collecting pure. The irrepressible Henry Mayhew provided this description of the unfortunate workers:

The pure-finder … is often found in the open streets as dogs wander where they like. The pure-finders always carry a handle basket, generally with a cover, to hide the contents, and have their right hand covered with a black leather glove; many of them however dispense with the glove, as they say it is much easier to wash their hands than to keep the glove fit for use. Thus equipped, they may be seen pursuing their avocation in almost every street in and about London, excepting such streets as are now cleansed by the 'street orderlies' of whom the pure-finders grievously complain, as being an unwarrantable interference in the privileges of their class.

Queen's Hall

Langham Place

THE ORIGINAL HOME OF THE 'PROMS', QUEEN'S Hall opened in 1893 but was not an initial success.

Containing two auditoria – one with seating for 2500 and the other a smaller room for chamber orchestras and an audience of 500 – in particular, its décor did not immediately strike a chord with music lovers.

The architect, T E Knightly, had insisted that the main ceiling should be painted the same colour as the belly of a London mouse, and is said to have hung a strip of the same in the painter's workshop to facilitate an accurate match. However, if the interior design left a little to be desired, the acoustics were superb. The walls were covered in wood paneling that was separated from the stone work by batons, covered with stretched cloth and sealed, achieving its designer's aim of resonating like a violin.

When Henry Wood started his Promenade concerts in 1895, it proved a turning point for the hall, which over time was to become known as the 'musical centre for the Empire'. Nonetheless, its cramped seating came in for much criticism well into the 20th century. In 1913, for instance, the *Musical Times* commented:

In the placing of the seats, apparently no account whatever is taken even of the average length of lower limbs, and it appeared to be the understanding … that legs were to be left in the cloak room.

At two pence apiece this would be expensive, and there might be difficulties afterwards if the cloak room sorting arrangements were not perfect.

Fortunately, the seating arrangements were significantly improved during a rejig shortly before the First World War and the hall went from strength to strength. In the 1930s it became the base for both the London Philharmonic Orchestra and the BBC Symphony Orchestra, with many of the period's greatest musicians playing here, including Richard Strauss, Maurice Ravel, Edward Elgar and Claude Debussy. Indeed, competition between the rival orchestras did much to raise the standard of classical music playing in Great Britain.

The Proms, supported by the BBC which was based nearby, were by then a fixture at Queen's Hall and the highlight of the classical music calendar. The outbreak of the Second World War put an end to that though, with the BBC withdrawing its staff to Bristol and the last Proms concert at Queen's Hall going ahead in 1940. In April 1941, an incendiary device completely gutted the main auditorium and it was deemed too expensive to rebuild. The Proms subsequently moved to the Royal Albert Hall, while Queen's Hall was demolished and the site redeveloped.

Rainbow Coffee House

Fleet Street

The Rainbow had been a tavern until its enterprising landlord, Mr Farr, started selling the new drink in the 1650s.

Arousing much jealously from vintners who in 1657 accused him of causing 'Disorders and Annoys'. In their indictment, they referred to 'James Farr. A barber, for makinge and selling a drink called coffee, whereby in makinge the same, he annoyeth his neighbours by evil smells'. Nonetheless, Farr persisted in his enterprise, the Arabic drink becoming increasingly popular all the way through to today. The Rainbow, however, was demolished in 1859.

Ranelagh Gardens

Chelsea

'Ah! Ranelagh was a noble place! Such taste! Such elegance! And such beauty!'

So said William Hone in his *Table-Book* in 1829. Located two miles outside of London in the grounds of Ranelagh House in what was then the village of Chelsea, it briefly eclipsed Vauxhall (another of the capital's fashionable pleasure gardens) as the most exclusive haunt of the wealthy.

Ranelagh Gardens opened to the public in 1742 and its chief attraction was a Rotunda that boasted a 185ft circumference and resembled the Pantheon in Rome. Its interior was elegantly decorated and when well-lit and full of company, it was thought unequalled in 'Europe for beauty, elegance and grandeur'. It was heated by equipment hidden by its arches, porticoes, niches and paintings. The ceiling was decorated with celestial figures, festoons of flowers and arabesque, all lit by a circle of chandeliers.

Masquerades were the order of the day at Ranelagh and were often attended by the entire royal family donning disguises. Horace Walpole's description of the Jubilee Masquerade in 1749 captures the essence of the occasion:

It was by far the best understood and prettiest spectacle I ever saw – nothing in a fairy tale ever surpassed it. One of the proprietors, who is a German, and belongs to court, had got my Lady Yarmouth to persuade the king to order it ... When you entered, you found the whole garden filled with marquees and spread with tents, which remained all night very commodely. In one quarter was a May-pole, dressed with garlands, and people dancing round it to a tabour and pipe, and rustic music, all masked, as were all the various bands of music that were disposed in different parts of the garden; some like huntsmen, with French horns; some like peasants; and a troop of harlequins and scaramouches in the little open temple on the mount. On the canal was a sort of gondola, adorned with flags and streamers, and filled with music, rowing about. All round the outside of the amphitheatre were shops, filled with Dresden china, japan, &c., and all the shopkeepers in masks; the amphitheatre was

illuminated, and in the middle was a circular bower, composed of all kinds of firs, in tubs, from twenty to thirty feet high; under them orange trees, with small lamps in each orange, and below them all sorts of auriculas in pots; and festoons of natural flowers hanging from tree to tree. Between the arches, too, were firs, and smaller ones in the balconies above. There were booths for tea and wine, gaming-tables and dancing, and about two thousand persons present. In short, it pleased me more than the finest thing I ever saw.

Caneletto's painting of the Rotunda's interior in 1751 marked the beginning of the venue's heyday, which peaked in the 1780s. But its wildly popular exotic masquerades were to prove its downfall, as they acquired a reputation for immorality and became less and less frequented by people of rank and fashion. By 1800 Ranelagh was struggling to make ends meet, as Vauxhall Pleasure Gardens across the river once again drew the fashionable crowd. The last masquerade was held in 1803 and the much-loved Rotunda was demolished in 1805.

Sir Richard Phillips returned to the scene of the now abandoned Gardens in 1817 and wrote:

No glittering lights! No brilliant happy company! no peals of laughter from thronged boxes! no chorus of a hundred instruments and voices! All was death-like stillness! Is such, I exclaimed, the end of human splendour ? … I was myself one of three thousand of the gayest mortals ever assembled in one of the gayest scenes which the art of man could devise—ay, on this very spot; yet the whole is now changed into the dismal scene of desolation before me!

Today the old grounds are home to the Chelsea Hospital.

Ratcliffe Highway

Wapping

Running east from the Tower of London to Limehouse, the ill-fated Ratcliffe Highway became so notorious that its name was twice changed in an attempt to salvage its reputation.

This ancient road was originally built by the Romans and connected the city to the village of Ratcliffe (or Red Cliff), which by 1600 had been swallowed up by urban and dockside development. The area around the road was famous for its maritime community and by the 17th century had an earthy reputation. *The Gentleman's Magazine* once described its population as 'dissolute sailors, blackmailing wharfmen, rowdy fishermen, audacious highwaymen, sneak thieves and professional cheats'.

By 1850, the highway had become the 'Regent Street of seamen', according to Walter Thornbury. It had shops specializing in selling wild animals, it was not unusual to see tigers, lions and pelicans as you walked along its length. On one occasion, a tiger escaped and grabbed a small boy in its jaws before making-off down Commercial Road. A passerby took up a crowbar to free the poor infant from the animal's jaws, but his blow only succeeded in killing the child.

Yet it was another incident that sealed Ratcliffe Highway's infamy. On Saturday, 7 December 1811, Margaret Jewell, a housemaid, returned to her employer's shop after buying oysters for their supper. Unable to open the door of 29 Ratcliffe Highway and finding the house in darkness, she called for assistance. When the door was forced, the bodies of Timothy Marr, his wife and their baby, plus a shop assistant, were discovered. They had been brutally murdered, their throats cuts.

Panic spread like wildfire and the government offered a reward of 500 guineas for the arrest of the perpetrator. Nonetheless, just twelve days later another killing spree took place at the King's Arms public house on nearby Gravel Pit Lane, running from Ratcliffe Highway towards the river. The landlord – a man named Williamson – his wife and a barmaid had all had their throats cut too. An apprentice, John Turner, discovering the murderer at his work, only escaped by running away, locking himself in his room and climbing out of a window, using his bed sheets as a rope. Shortly afterwards, a man named Williams, a former shipmate of Marr's, was arrested and imprisoned at Coldbath Fields.

The effect of these grisly murders should not be underestimated. Not only did Ratcliffe Highway receive a new name (it was first renamed as St George's Street and became The Highway in 1937) but public outrage was such that it led to significant pressure for a full-time police service.

The murderer, Williams, committed suicide before he could be brought to justice but to satisfy the public, his body was dragged through the streets on an open cart to the site of both sets of murders, then on to the crossroads of New Road and Canon Street Road. There a hole was dug and his body cast in. Hundreds watched as a stake was driven through his heart before he was buried.

Rillington Place

Ladbroke Grove

THIS HUMBLE SITE WAS NOT ONLY THE SCENE OF a number of grisly murders but earned a notable place in British judicial history.

For No 10 Rillington Place was the home of John Reginald Christie and it was here that he murdered seven women, including his wife, and a baby.

Christie's bizarre sexual murders shocked the nation upon their discovery in 1953 by new tenants who moved in to the premises after Christie had left. They found three bodies hidden in an alcove in the kitchen, covered over with wallpaper. Christie's wife was later found under the floorboards of the front room, while the bodies of two other women were unearthed in the tiny garden.

Adding to the horror of the situation was the knowledge that three years previously, Christie had given evidence at the murder trial of Timothy Evans, who was convicted of killing his daughter, Geraldine Evans. It was a murder of which it would become apparent that Christie himself was guilty. The Evans family had shared the house with the Christies, who lived in the downstairs flat.

Claiming medical knowledge, Christie had offered to perform an abortion on Timothy's wife, Beryl (abortions being illegal in the UK at the time). With her husband absent, Beryl was gassed, raped and strangled by Christie. He told Timothy that his wife had died when the operation went wrong and persuaded Evans to abscond. The Evans' young daughter, Geraldine, would be looked after by a couple who lived nearby, Christie assured him. The troubled Evans soon surrendered himself to police in Wales and it was apparent that he had no knowledge yet that his daughter was also dead.

A terrible miscarriage of justice was about to take place as police botched a search of Rillington Place. While they turned up the corpses of Evans' wife and child, they failed, for instance, to uncover the bodies of Ruth Fuerst and Muriel Eady buried in the garden, even though a thigh bone was propped up against the fence. Evans signed a 'confession' for the murders of Beryl and Geraldine that he later retracted and which was almost certainly concocted by police. Despite this and worries about Evans' mental capacities, he was convicted at the Old Bailey of the murder of his baby daughter, the star witness for the prosecution being John Christie.

Three years passed before Christie murdered his own wife in December 1952, then three other women in January, February and March of 1953. He used the domestic gas supply to ensure that they were unconscious before raping and strangling them with a rope. Despite the suspicions of his wife's relatives, Christie sub-let his flat and took rooms in King's Cross under his own name. The bodies were discovered on 24 March and Christie was arrested on Putney Bridge a week later.

Confessing to the murders, he pleaded insanity but was found guilty and hanged at Pentonville Prison on 15 July. Following his execution, a campaign was started to clear Timothy Evans, who was eventually posthumously pardoned in 1966 by Roy Jenkins, the then Home Secretary. His case contributed to the parliamentary campaign for the abolition of hanging in 1965.

As for Rillington Place, it was renamed Ruston Close, and No 10 was demolished in the 1970s as part of the Westway development scheme. The residents of Ruston Mews, W11, are often keen to point out that their street is not the site of these terrible crimes.

Rivers

Apart from the aforementioned Effra and Fleet, there are a number of other lost or subterranean rivers in London. These include:

The Neckinger – a small stream in Bermondsey, close to the medieval abbey. It may have derived its name from being an ancient site of execution ('the Devil's Neck Tie' being a term for hangman's noose). It formed part of the boundary of Jacob's Island, immortalised as the home of Fagin in Dickens's *Oliver Twist*, and is still visible as it enters into the Thames at St Saviour's Dock.

The Peck – providing the root of the name Peckham, this river ran from Forest Hill and emptied into the Thames at Rotherhithe.

The Tyburn – giving its name to London's historical site of executions, this stream once provided water for the city's populace via a three-mile tube called the Great Conduit, which ran from Marble Arch to East Cheap. Its waters once filled the ponds in St James's Park and its ancient course formed part of the boundary of Thorney Island.

The Walbrook (Walbrook Street, City of London) – thought to be the original source of water for the Roman city.

The Westbourne – giving its name to Westbourne Park, this river used to flow into the Serpentine in Hyde Park. Now a sewer, it can be seen in a large pipe running over the Circle and District Line platforms at Sloane Square Station.

The Rookeries

A GENERIC NAME USED FOR A NUMBER OF
terrible slums in London during the Victorian
era. Etymologically, it is derived from one of two
associations with the rook, a bird of the crow family.

It may relate to the habit of rooks of nesting in large and noisy communities called rookeries, or perhaps it is a play on words, with 'rooking' a slang term for thieving that dates from the 16th century and which supposedly reflects another trait of the bird.

London's most notorious Rookery was at St Giles, which spread from St Martin's Lane up to where the Centre Point office block is today and included the area of Seven Dials. Irish immigrants flocked to London seeking employment in the early part of the 1800s, with many of them settling in the squalid tenements of St Giles so that it became known as 'Little Dublin' or 'The Holy Land'. But holy it was not.

Poverty forced many families to share their rooms, with up to seventeen people per room sleeping in shifts. Although many of the residents were undoubtedly honest and hard-working, the area's run-down buildings and warren-like alleys encouraged a mood of lawlessness. Police hardly dared venture in and the Rookery served as a home for thieves, prostitutes and assorted low-life for many years.

Charles Dickens visited one night in the interests of research (he was accompanied by five policemen) and used the experience to great effect in a number of his novels. For

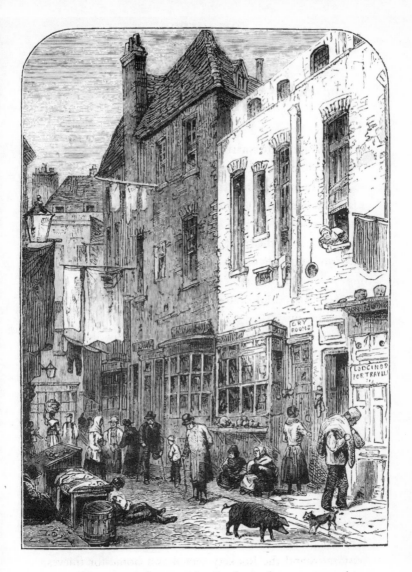

many Victorian reformers, the Rookeries became something of an obsession, and Charles Booth's Map of London Poverty describing the area, which he coloured black, as home to 'the lowest class ... street sellers, loafers and criminals'.

Aside from St Giles, the city's other Rookeries included Westminster, Rosemary Lane (see entry below) and Jacob's Island in Bermondsey. The improving Victorians, desperate to rid the capital of these abominations, came up with plans that saw New Oxford Street and Victoria Street driven through the heart of these slum areas. Their schemes were successful to a degree for the Rookeries are no more. But even 150 years later, these new roads may still be said to lack – for want of a better word – soul, perhaps because they came at considerable expense to the once thriving communities they destroyed by their construction.

Rosemary Lane

Tower Hill

AN ANCIENT STREET HARD BY THE TOWER OF London, this was for centuries the home of the Rag Fair, an open market that specialized in the selling of old clothes for the poor of London.

The area was a labyrinth of lanes and alleys, its cramped housing giving refuge to the poor and destitute. Henry Mayhew described it as the lowest part of London, inhabited by 'dredgers, ballast-heavers, coal-whippers, watermen, lumpers, &c., as well as the slop-workers and "sweaters" from the glassworks in the Minories'. Nonetheless, it was to here that the majority of London's labourers came to buy their clothes. Indeed, George Godwin, writing in *London Shadows* (1852), found at the Rag Fair all the items a bride might need for her wedding day:

> *A shift…..1d*
> *A pair of stays….. 2d*
> *A flannel petticoat…..4d*
> *A black Orleans ditto…..4d*
> *A pair of white cotton stockings…..1d*
> *A very good light-coloured cotton gown…..10d*
> *A pair of single-soled slippers, with spring heels…..2d*
> *A double-dyed bonnet, including a neat cap…..2d*
> *A pair of white cotton gloves…..1d*
> *A lady's green silk paletot, lined with crimson silk,*
>   *trimmed with black…..10d*
> *[Total] …..3s. 1d.*

Among Rosemary Lane's most famous residents was Richard Brandon, the executioner of Charles I, who lived and died here. The area also birthed a religion in the 1650s, of which the artist William Blake was reportedly a follower. Muggletonianism was founded by two tailors, John Reeve and Lodowicke Muggleton, who claimed to be the last prophets from the Book of Revelations. Despite the two being whipped and pilloried on the orders of Oliver Cromwell, their religion survived until at least the 1970s, when the group's last trustee, Philip Noakes, died and bequeathed its archive to the British Library.

Much of the hodge-podge of housing that made up Rosemary Lane was destroyed during the coming of the railways and what remained was renamed Royal Mint Street.

St George's Fields

Southwark

**ST GEORGE'S FIELDS WAS A LARGE AREA OF OPEN LAND
south of the river between Lambeth and Southwark,
which was once the destination of choice for London's
working people who couldn't afford the more
salubrious resorts at Ranelagh or Vauxhall Gardens.**

Often flooded when the Thames tide was at its highest,
the Romans had started to ditch and drain the land as far
back as the 3rd century. The diarists Samuel Pepys and John
Evelyn both described how city-dwellers camped out here
with what remained of their property after the Great Fire in
1666. But the area is most famous for the St George's Field's
Massacre, which occurred on 10 May 1768. When a crowd
of Londoners came to free a radical MP, John Wilkes, from
King's Bench Prison, troops opened fire on them, killing
seven. Then twelve years later, in 1780, a reported 50,000
people gathered here at the beginning of what became
known as the Gordon Riots, which lasted for nearly a week
and cost 850 lives. In 1812, James Smith wrote the following
lines about the locality:

> *Saint George's fields are fields no more;*
> *The trowel supersedes the plough;*
> *Swamps huge and inundate of yore,*
> *Are changed to civic villas now.*

Today the fields are completely built over, with St

George's Circus, which leads to the Elephant and Castle, the only reminder of these vast meadows where Londoners used to collect herbs and watercress.

St Paul's Cathedral

SIR CHRISTOPHER WREN'S ICONIC BUILDING WAS actually the fifth church to be built on this site. The original was constructed in 604 AD by Mellitus, with permission from Ethelbert, King of Kent.

It was rumoured that it had been built on an ancient Roman temple to Diana, though the theory was disproved by Wren when he was digging the foundations for his cathedral. Although he unearthed the remains of a Roman burial site at a depth of 18 feet, it was the Roman custom to bury their dead outside of their city walls, effectively ruling out the presence of a temple at this location.

A second wooden church burnt down here in 962 and a stone one was built to replace it, but fire struck again and razed that building in 1087. It was then that the building of 'Old St Paul's' began. This project was also beset by blazes – another fire destroyed much work in 1136 – and the church was not completed until 1314. Once finished, it was the third largest cathedral in Europe, with a spire rising 149 metres.

Like many religious buildings of the time, it contained a collection of holy relics purportedly including the arms of Mellitus (which were of different sizes), some hair from Mary

Magdalene, the blood of St Paul, the milk of the Virgin, the hand of St John, pieces of the skull of Thomas à Becket, and the head and jaw of King Ethelbert.

During a great storm in 1561, the spire was struck by lightning and caught alight. The flames burned furiously downwards for four hours and the bells melted, lead poured down in torrents and the roof fell in. The cathedral stood in ruins but within a month a false roof was erected and by the end of the year, the aisles were leaded in. The spire, however, was never re-erected.

As London's mother church, St Paul's was always at the centre of life in the metropolis, although not always in a way that the faithful appreciated. For instance, the Catholic Queen Mary issued an act that forbade the carrying of beer casks and baskets of bread, fish, flesh, or fruit, or leading mules or horses through the cathedral, under pain of fines and imprisonment. Later, Elizabeth I issued a proclamation forbidding affray or the drawing of swords in the church, or shooting a hand-gun within the church or churchyard, under threat of two months' imprisonment. Soon afterwards, a man who provoked an affray here was set in the pillory in the churchyard and had his ears nailed to a post before they were cut off.

Others met even more severe fates in the church grounds, including four of the Gunpowder Plotters (Digby, Winter, Grant and Bates), who were hung, drawn and quartered here in January 1606. By that time, the building was in a sorry state of repair. Charles I would commission Inigo Jones to carry out extensive repairs but balked at the estimated £22,000 costs, then unwisely allowed his favourite, the Duke of Buckingham, to take the stone collected for rebuilding to raise his own palace on the Strand.

St Paul's was further degraded when Parliamentary soldiers were billeted here. Treating it with little respect, they had to be banned from playing skittles inside, except between the hours of 6 and 9pm. After the Restoration, Wren was invited to submit plans for its rebuilding even before the Great Fire occurred. But the 1666 conflagration completely gutted the dilapidated structure, melting the six acres of lead that covered the roof. John Evelyn's diary records stones falling from the walls in great cascades and although parts of the structure were considered salvageable, the remains were eventually demolished. Starting from a blank canvas, Wren built the beautiful edifice we have today. Wren once said 'I build for eternity' and we must hope that is the case, given the cathedral's fiery history.

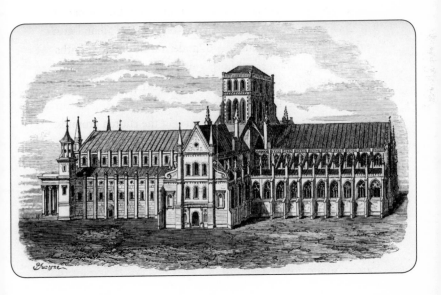

Salmon's Waxworks

Fleet Street

ORIGINALLY SITED AT THE GOLDEN BALL ON
St Martin's Le Grand, Mrs Salmon's Waxworks – a
precursor to Madame Tussauds, which opened in
1702 – moved to Fleet Street in 1711.

William Hogarth was a regular visitor, as was James Boswell. The collection, which filled six rooms, included likenesses of the kings and queens of England as well as galleries of horrors, myths and the fantastic.

An advertisement for Mrs Salmon's Waxworks ran in *Tatler* and specified such attractions as 'the Turkish Seraglio in wax-work', 'the Fatal Sisters that spin, reel, and cut the thread of man's life' and 'an Old Woman flying from Time, who shakes his head and hour-glass with sorrow at seeing age so unwilling to die'. 'Nothing but life can exceed the motions of the heads, hands, eyes, etc. of these figures,' the ad assured the reader.

Following Mrs Salmon's death, the exhibition was run by a surgeon named Clarke. Some of the exhibits were especially grotesque, such as that depicting the execution of Charles I and another showing 'Margaret, Countess of Heninburgh, lying on a bed of State, with her Three Hundred and Sixty Five Children, all born at one birth'.

Moving to the south side of Fleet Street in 1795, the attraction survived well into the Victorian era. Its last location on Fleet Street can still be seen, though today it is the Prince Henry's Room museum at No 17.

Silvertown Explosives Factory

West Ham

19 January 1917 saw the biggest explosion in London's history at the Brunner Mond chemical factory at Silvertown, on the northern bank of the Thames in West Ham.

The factory had manufactured caustic soda since it opened in 1893 but with Britain's Great War effort hampered by a shortage of high explosives, the government ordered Brunner Mond to start making and refining trinitrotoluene (TNT), despite the factory being in a heavily built-up area. Production started in 1915 and by the time of the accident, the factory was processing 9 tons a day.

At 6.52, a small fire broke out, which ignited 50 tons of TNT. The explosion wrought immense devastation, destroying the factory and surrounding warehouses, completely razing 900 houses to the ground and damaging some 70,000 others. Across the river, at the site of today's O2 (formerly the Millennium Dome), a gasometer containing 7 million cubic feet of gas ignited. The blaze was seen as far away as Guildford and the blast was audible a hundred miles away in Sussex and Norfolk. Seventy-three people were killed in the disaster.

Slang

LONDONERS HAVE ALWAYS HAD A WAY WITH WORDS.
We owe a great debt for some wonderful phrases
and words that are no longer in common use, and
which also tell us much of the habits, street life and
prejudices of the times.

Academy A brothel
Acorn The Gallows, from 'riding the horse sired from an acorn'
Apple dumpling shop A woman's breasts
Beggar's bullets Stones, for throwing at the wealthy
Blindman's holiday Night or darkness
Blue skin Mixed race
Botch A tailor
To box a Jesuit To masturbate
Catch Fart A footman, catching his master's farts
Dead Chelsea By God! A soldier would shout this after receiving a
    wound in battle, a reference to the military hospital there.
Chummage Paid by rich prisoners to make their roommates
    sleep elsewhere, for example, on the stairs
City college Newgate Prison
Clapham A sexually transmitted disease, 'he went out by
    Had'em, and came round by Clapham home'
Corinthians Those who visit brothels
Covent Garden Ague Sexually Transmitted Disease
Covent Garden Nun A prostitute
Deadly Nevergreen The gallows, bearing grisly fruit all year round

Derrick *The hangman, sometime thought to have given his name to modern-day derricks, lifting mechanisms used at ports etc*

Dick *During the reign of Queen Dick, that is never*

Doll *A Bartholomew doll – a slutty over-dressed woman, like the toys sold at Bartholomew Fair*

Drury Lane Vestal *A prostitute, after the area, formally a major location of the sex trade*

Earth Bath *The grave*

English Burgundy *Porter – a stout invented in London*

Execution day *The day you do the washing*

Farting Crackers *Trousers*

Feague *To feague a horse was to stick ginger, or a live eel, up its rectum to make it appear frisky before selling it*

Friday Face *During Cromwell's time it was compulsory to fast on Fridays, a habit that continued after the reformation – hence Friday face*

St Giles' Greek *The language of thieves and gypsies, who were mainly said to live in the St Giles area of London*

Greenwich barbers *The men who dig sand in Greenwich, from their habit of shaving off the sandbanks*

Hasty pudding *A poor road 'The way through Wandsworth is quite a hasty pudding'*

Holborn Hill *Riding backwards up Holborn Hill, to go to the gallows, on the way to Tyburn*

Hopping Giles *Being disabled, St Giles was the patron saint of the disabled*

Irish beauty *A woman with two black eyes*

Job's Dock *The ward for venereal disease at St Barts*

Laystall *Dunghills of human waste*

Lily White *Chimney sweeps*

Lion *Sending lads to see the lions washed at Tower ditch was a longstanding April fools joke for city dwellers. Sticking two fingers up someone's nose and pulling was said to make a lion of them*

Little Barbary *The village of Wapping*

Little ease *An ancient prison cell in the Guildhall, being so low that a lad could not stand in it, hence little ease*

Long Meg *After the famous tall woman of Westminster, Long Meg became a sarcastic term for any female of height*

Maccaroni *A fop or dandy. Returning from the Grand Tour with a taste for all thing Italian – food, clothing and hair – maccaroni's strutted around the city*

Milk the pigeon *To attempt the impossible*

Monkey *Using a long straw or tube to illicitly drink wine or other booze from a cask was said to be 'sucking the monkey'*

Mooncurser *Link boys, who used to provide light to walk citizens home before the advent of street lighting, were said to be mooncursers, as the moon did them out of work*

Nappy house *A brothel*

Neck Verse *A convict could escape execution by claiming Benefit of the Clergy, which meant in practice reading in Latin the first verse of Psalm 51*

Nit Squeezer *A hairdresser*

Noll *Oliver Cromwell, Old Noll*

Nutcrackers *The pillory*

Nypper *Someone who cut purses, which used to be worn on a string from the clothing*

Oliver's skull *A chamber pot*

Paddington fair day *A hanging day, Tyburn being in the parish of Paddington*

Paviour's workshop *The street*

Picture frame The sheriff's picture frame – the gallows or the pillory

Piss pot hall A house in Clapton, Hackney, built by a maker of chamber pots

Polish the king's iron To be imprisoned was said to be polishing the king's iron, to be in fetters

Porridge island An area inhabited by cooks in the alleyway leading from St Martin's churchyard

Queer plungers People who threw themselves in the Thames to be rescued by a friend and taken to the Humane Society, who paid for the rescue of the destitute

Riding St George Having sex with the lady on top, riding on the dragon as it were, said to be a good way of conceiving a bishop

Romeville London

Rushers A class of thieves who knocked on the doors of the wealthy, knowing them to be away, and when the door was opened, rushing in and taking the valuables

On St Geoffrey's day Never, there is no St Geoffrey

Salesman's dog Someone employed to bark out the wares of a shopkeeper

Schism shop A meeting house of dissenters

Scotch warming pan A fart, or a woman

Sharks The very highest rank of pickpockets

Sidepocket Wanting something unnecessary – 'he needs it like a dog needs a sidepocket'

Silver laced Replete with lice

Smithfield bargain A marriage undertaken purely for the profit of one of the party, Smithfield was where women were reputedly sold like cattle

Tangerines Debtors at Newgate, so called because they were housed in a room called *Tangier Thames*

The impossible *He'll find no way to set the Thames on fire*

Three penny upright *A prostitute who charges three pence, and has sex while standing up*

Tom turdman *The man who collects night soil*

Tom of Bedlam *A lunatic, Shakespeare's Poor Tom from* King Lear

Touch bone and whistle *Anyone who has farted may be pinched and punched, until he has touched bone (the teeth) and whistled*

Tower Hill play *A kick in the bum and a slap in the face*

Vice Admiral of the narrow seas *A man who, when drunk, pisses under the table in his neighbour's shoes*

Vowel *To vowel is to pay one's gambling debts with and I.O.U.*

Walking up against the wall *To run up a tab in a boozer, where one's tally was often chalked up on the wall*

Wasp *A prostitute with a venereal disease, so called because of the sting in her tail*

Westminster wedding *When a rogue marries a whore*

Windward Passage *Homosexual, one who navigates by the Windward Passage*

Zed *A crocked or deformed person, shaped like the letter*

Steelyard

Cannon Street

DEMOLISHED IN 1865 TO MAKE WAY FOR
Cannon Street Railway Station, the Steelyard was
an autonomous enclave of German merchants who
controlled much of London's trade with the Hanseatic
League, a group of German ports that banded together
in mutual self-protection against Baltic Sea piracy.

First recorded in the city in 1157, the German traders were
granted freedom from taxation under a charter of Richard I in
1197. They expanded their property over the next 200 years
and in 1598 John Stow described their premises and trade in
his *Survey of London*:

*The hall is large, built of stone, with three arched gates
towards the street, the middlemost whereof is far bigger than the
others, and is seldom opened; the other two be secured up. The
same is now called the old hall. The merchants of Almaine used to
bring hither as well wheat, rye, and other grain, as cables, ropes,
masts, pitch, tar, flax, hemp, linen cloth, wainscots, wax, steel,
and other profitable merchandise.*

The German merchants kept themselves to themselves,
drinking their own Rhenish wine, enforcing a self-imposed
curfew and forbidding their women to mix with the locals.
But this independence and separation aroused suspicion and
jealousy. Furthermore, their control of much of the lucrative
English wool trade angered rival London merchants who

petitioned the Crown to take action.

In 1551 Edward VI attempted to restrict their trade, and they were banished by Elizabeth I in 1598 but returned under James I with much reduced privileges. The Steelyard was completely destroyed in 1666 by the Great Fire but was rebuilt afterwards, a German trading presence remaining in the city until the 1850s. The name Steelyard arose from one of two possible sources – either the measuring scales used to weigh goods coming into the port, or directly from the German word *Stalhof.*

Street Cries

BEFORE THE ADVENT OF GLASS-FRONTED SHOPS,
much of the city's trade was carried out by hawkers
wandering the streets.

They sold anything and everything, and to attract attention they all had their own cries. Here is a selection taken from Charles Hindley's 1884 work, *A History of the Cries of London, Ancient and Modern*:

- *All that has to complain of corns! As fast as the shoe maker lames you I'll cure you, you'll not have to take the bus home when you've used my corn salve!*
- *Any hareskins cook? Hareskins!*
- *Buy my diddle dumplings hot hot diddle diddle diddle dumplings hot*
- *Catch 'em alive, only half a penny! (fly paper man)*
- *Chairs to mend, old chairs to mend if I had the money I could spend I would never cry old chairs to mend*
- *Cherries a ha'penny a stick come and pick come and pick! Cherries big as plums who come who comes?*
- *Chestnuts all 'ot, a penny a score!*
- *Dog's meat! cat's Cat's meat! Nice tripe! Neat's feet! Come and buy my trotters!*
- *Fresh wo-orter creases!*
- *Ha-a-aandsome cod! Best in the markets! All alive alive o*
- *Had had had had had haddick! All fresh and good*
- *Here's all hot pies! Toss and buy! Up and win'em!*
- *Hot spiced ginger bread! Buy my spiced ginger bread! Smo-o-oking hot!*
- *Hot spiced gingerbread nuts, nuts, nuts! If one'll warm you, wha-at'll a pound do? Wha-a-a-at'll a pound do?*
- *Now or never! Whelk! Whelk! Whelk!*
- *'old your horse sir?*
- *Round and sound, two pence a pound, cherries rare ripe cherries*
- *Three a penny Yarmouth bloaters*

- *Who will buy a new love song? Only a ha'penny!*
- *Who'll buy a bonnet for fourpence?*
- *Wi-ild Hampshire rabbits, 2 a shilling*
- *Young lambs to sell, young lams to sell, molly and dolly Richard and nell, buy my youngd lambs and I'll use you well*

Street Traders

IN HIS EXHAUSTIVE WORK *LONDON LABOUR and the London Poor*, Henry Mayhew listed the various types of street traders he had discovered making a precarious living in the capital.

His list is huge, with some of the professions still active today, though thankfully some have long gone.

TYPES OF STREET SELLERS

Green Stuff	Pea soup and hot eels
Pickled whelks	Fried fish
Sheep's trotters	Baked potatoes
Ham sandwiches	Bread
Hot green peas	Cat and dogs meat
Coffee stall keepers	Ginger beer, sherbert and lemonade
Milk	Curds and whey
Rice milk	Water carriers
Pastry and confectionary	Piemen
Boiled pudding	Plum duff
Cakes and tarts	Gingerbread nuts

RIPE CHERRIES   WATER CRESSES   DOLLS TO SELL   GREEN CABBAGES

Hot cross and Chelsea buns	Muffin and crumpets
Cough drops	Ice and ice creams
Corn salve	Crackers and detonating balls
Cigar lights and fuzees	Gutta percha heads
Fly paper and beetle wafers	Walking sticks and whips
Pipes, snuff and tobacco	Cigars
Sponge	Washleather
Spectacles and eyeglasses	Dolls
Poison for rats	Second-hand musical instruments
Second-hand weapons	Second-hand telescopes
Live animals	Dogs
Live birds	Birds' nests
Gold and silver fish	Coals
Coke	Shells

STREET TRADES

Screeves – writers of begging letters and petitions

Dog finders	Pure finders
Cigar-end finders	Old wood gatherers

IMAGES MILK GIRL BONNET BOX FLOWER GIRL

Dredgers and river finders Sewer hunters
Mudlarks Dustmen
Chimney sweeps Rat catchers
Crossing sweepers Bug destroyers
Garret masters Doll's eye makers
Coal heavers Coal backers
Ballast getters Ballast heavers

TYPES OF STREET ENTERTAINERS

Punch and Judy men Strong men
Exhibitor of mechanical figures Jugglers
Telescope exhibitor Conjurors
Street clowns Silly Billy
Ballet performers Stilt vaulters
Street photographers Penny profile cutters
Writer without hands Chalker on flag stones
Exhibitor of birds and mice Snake, sword and knife
Fantoccini man (puppet man) swallowers

Tabard Inn

Borough

In The Canterbury Tales, Geoffrey Chaucer
immortalized this inn as the starting place of
his journey:

In Southwerk at the Tabard as I lay
Redy to wenden on my pilgrymage
To Caunterbury with ful devout corage,
At nyght was come into that hostelrye

The Tabard was not only the most famous inn of London, it
was also the most famous in literature and hence maybe the
most famous pub in history.

Southwark, outside of the jurisdiction of the city, was
the jumping-off point for citizens travelling southwards from
the capital and contained a large number of coaching houses
where traders and pilgrims stayed before entering or leaving
the city. The Tabard was first mentioned in 1304, the land
having been purchased by the Abbot of Hyde to build himself
a house and a hostelry 'for the convenience of travelers'.

In *London Chaunticeres* (1659), the tapster of the inn
charmingly described his morning work: 'I have cut two
dozen of toste, broacht a new barrel of ale, washt all the cups
and flagons, made a fire i' the' George, drained all the beer
out of th' Half Moon the company left o' th' floore last night,
wip'd the tables, and have swept every room.' By then, the
Tabard was a galleried coaching house with many separate
rooms, hence 'the George' and 'th' Half Moon'. Other room

names known to have existed at the inn include 'Rose parlar', 'Clyff parlar', 'Crowne chamber', 'Keye chamber' and the 'Corne chamber'.

A tabard is a type of sleeveless coat but the name of the inn somehow changed – either through ignorance or design – to The Talbot (a breed of dog) sometime in the 17th century, after which time both names were commonly used to describe it. It burnt down in the great fire of Southwark that destroyed 500 properties in 1676 but was rebuilt on roughly the same plans and survived until 1875, when it was demolished.

Other famous coaching houses on Borough High Street included The White Hart (headquarters of Jack Cade's rebellion in 1450), The King's Head (formerly The Pope's Head but changed during the Reformation), The Queen's Head, The Bull, The Christopher and The Spurre. Fortunately, one side of The George remains to this day, providing a fine example of what London boozers must have once been like.

Thorney Island

Westminster

ORIGINALLY FORMED BY A LOOP OF THE THAMES and the division of the Tyburn River, this island may have been inhabited by the Romans.

King Offa (who died in 796) issued a charter describing it as a 'loco terribili' (or terrible place), its modern name deriving from the thorns that covered the area.

Perhaps keen to make use of existing Roman foundations, Sebert (540–616), an early Saxon convert to Christianity, chose the island as the site of his second church, the Minster in the West (hence Westminster). Early Christian legend has it that the night before the church was due to be consecrated it was visited by St Peter who:

…in an unknown garb, showed himself to a fisher on the Surrey side, and bade him carry him over, with promise of reward. The fisher complied, and saw his fare enter the new-built Church of Sebert, that suddenly seemed on fire, with a glow that enkindled the firmament. Meantime the heavenly host scattered sound and fragrance, the fisher of souls wrote upon the pavement the alphabet in Greek and Hebrew, in twelve places anointed the walls with the holy oil, lighted the tapers, sprinkled the water, and did all else needful for the dedication of a church.

The fishermen of the Thames were said to have been granted nets full of salmon as a reward, as long as they gave one-tenth to the new church.

This early building was subsequently destroyed by Vikings, but Edward the Confessor, England's penultimate Saxon King, built not only Westminster Abbey here but also a home, Westminster Palace, now better known as the Houses of Parliament. By the 12th century, much of the surrounding land had been cultivated and had lost its inhospitable reputation. It thus quickly developed as a centre of government, remaining so to this day.

With the land drained and the river covered over, Thorney Island (or the Isle of Thorns) has long since disappeared, although the name lives on in Thorney Street, which runs parallel to Millbank off Horseferry Road.

Toshers

THE GREAT STINK OF 1858, WHEN THERE WAS
so much human waste in the Thames that MPs
attended Parliament wearing handkerchiefs over
their faces to filter out the stench, led to a major
re-think of the capital's sewage system.

Over the next ten years, Sir Joseph Bazelgette oversaw a
massive sewer-building scheme that lay down over 2000 miles
of brick sewers and created embankments on both sides of
the Thames.

An unforeseen opportunity arose for impoverished city-
dwellers who were prepared to enter the sewers at the river-
side during low tide in search of old metal, coins, rags and
bone, to be sold later. The venerable Henry Mayhew recorded
their bizarre and unpleasant work, having interviewed several
of these men who called themselves toshers: 'Stories are told of
sewer hunters beset by myriads of enormous rats, and slaying
thousands of them in their struggle for life, till at length the
swarms of the savage things overpowered them, and in a few
days afterwards their skeletons were discovered picked to the
very bones.'

The toshers always travelled in groups of three or four
for protection, armed with a long rake which guarded against
vermin but which could also be used for pulling themselves out
when they became embedded in the 'mud'. These subterranean
travellers told stories of a mythical animal that ranged the
darkest passages – not unlike the stories of crocodiles in New

York's sewers – and many toshers believed a family of ferocious wild hogs resided in the sewers of Hampstead.

The income for the most successful practitioners of this dirty business was not inconsiderable, with Mayhew estimating the trade brought in around £20,000 in total each year – or a loss from each London home of 1s 4d.

Tyburn

Marble Arch

To CLOSE THE SCENE OF ALL HIS ACTIONS HE
Was brought from Newgate to the fatal tree;
And there his life resigned, his race is run,
And Tyburn ends what wickedness begun.

So went an old verse, for from 1300 until 1783 Tyburn was the foremost site of public execution in London. Named after the stream that ran nearby, most commentators place the site of the gallows at the junction of Edgware Road, Oxford Street and Bayswater Road. Today, a small stone plaque on the traffic island there commemorates the spot where approaching 50,000 criminals – from murderers to counterfeiters, thieves to traitors, rapists to religious offenders – met their ends, often in front of a large and rowdy crowd.

During the reign of Queen Elizabeth 1, the infamous Tyburn tree was erected. This awful device was triangular in construction, each of its three oak beams capable of hanging

eight miscreants – that is to say, twenty-four at once should the need arise. It was popularly known as the 'Triple Tree', 'the Deadly Never-green' and 'the Three-Legged Mare'.

Hanging days were virtually public holidays and such occasions became known as the Tyburn Fair. Thousands would line the streets from Newgate Prison to Tyburn to watch as the condemned were transported to their place of execution. At the hanging on 14 November 1724 of the notorious escapee, Jack Sheppard, it is thought that 200,000 people watched – equivalent to one-third of the capital's entire population at the time.

The phrase 'getting back on the wagon' – meaning never to drink again – arises from the journey made by the condemned along this route. At St Giles they were traditionally offered a bowl of wine – their last ever drink – before getting back on 'the wagon', a cart that was taking them to their death. The rope that was to hang them was already hung around their necks and their coffins lay at their feet.

At the place of execution, grandstands were built to

accommodate paying spectators, while ballad-singers played hurriedly penned songs about that day's criminals in the hope of earning a few pennies. Meanwhile, there was a thriving trade in 'penny bloods', one-page news sheets detailing the life histories, crimes and sometimes even the last words of the doomed. Hogarth depicted such a scene in plate 11 of *Industry and Idleness*.

The right of the condemned to speak their last free from the threat of any further punishment may well have been the tradition that led to the creation of Speakers' Corner. The last public hanging at Tyburn took place on 7 November 1783, when one John Austin was executed for highway robbery. A month later, public hanging resumed, but this time outside Newgate Prison.

Vauxhall Gardens

Lambeth

LET ME SIT AND SADLY PONDER
on the glories of Vauxhall;
Sink this mouldy mildewed present;
from its grave the past recall.
Is't the punch that stirs my fancy—
or the gooseberry champagne,
Sets phantasmal shapes careering
through the chambers of my brain?
PUNCH 1859

Early records show that in 1621 a manor house was owned by the Vaux family, who were successful vitners. By the 1660's the gardens surrounding 'Vaux Hall' were a popular resort for city dwellers. The season lasted from May until August, and guests would wander the site listening to the birds, sharing picnics and enjoying music, often also provided by the guests themselves.

Samuel Pepys visited numerous times during the period he kept his diary – between 1660 and 1669. He first visited in 1662, but under his entry for 28 May, 1667 he writes *'Went by water to Fox (sic) Hall, and there walked in Spring Gardens. A great deal of company; the weather and gardens pleasant, and cheap going thither: for a man may go to spend what he will, or nothing at all: all is one. But to hear the nightingale and other birds, and here fiddles and there a harp, and here a Jew's harp, and there laughing, and there [to see] fine people walking, is very diverting.'*

One of the main attractions of the gardens was their appeal for those wishing to meet members of the opposite sex – the long arbours and walk-ways were perfect for hiding from anxious parents. It soon however became a resort of prostitutes. In 1712, Sir Roger de Coverley, was interrupted by one such, during a leisurely stroll in the moonlight. She invited him to buy her a bottle of ale, and his reply was that 'She was a wanton Baggage, and bid her go about her Business.' He complained on leaving that he would rather 'if there were more Nightingales, and fewer Strumpets'.

Running for nearly 200 years, and through the reigns of ten monarchs, its greatest period was during the management of Jonathan Tyers, from 1727 until his death

in 1767. His best-known events were a series of 'Ridotto al Fresco', which were masked balls.

Vauxhall remained a fashionable venue, hosting the latest musicians and contemporary theatre, redesigning its gardens as taste and style demanded until the end of the 18th century when its popularity faltered.

The opening of Nine Elms railway terminus in 1838 effectively ended the gardens rural seclusion. The very last night of opening was 25 July 1859, the land being sold off for building development that was to devour rural south London over the next fifty years.

Walbrook

THE RIVER WAS THE SOURCE OF FRESH WATER FOR the Romans when they founded the city. It rose in Finsbury, ran along the route of Curtain Road and Apollo Street, through Bank and into the Thames at the site of today's Cannon Street Station.

It was too narrow and shallow to be used for navigation, although excavation has revealed a Roman wooden dock where it entered the Thames. Its route to the river after passing Bank is remembered in a nearby eponymous street name.

It was long suspected that the Romans built a temple here on its banks, and in 1889 a relief of the god Mithras was discovered – he is shown slaying a bull. At the same time a statue of a reclining river god was also found, 20 feet deep. The area was devastated by Second World War bombing and further discoveries were made in 1954.

Records show that by the late 13th century the river was so filthy that city officials decreed it must be 'made free from dung and other nuisances'. One hundred years later it was again reported to be totally blocked by rubbish thrown in by residents who lived along its banks. When St Margarets Lothbury was rebuilt in 1440 much of the river was covered over on orders of the Lord Mayor, Robert Lange, who paid for much of the work. By the time John Stow published his seminal *Survey of London* in 1598, the river had gone and Stow says 'the course of Walbrook is now hidden underground, and thereby hardly known'.

Watermen

THE THAMES WAS THE MAIN THOROUGHFARE
of London until the modern period of bridge
building that started after the construction of
Westminster Bridge in 1750.

Unregulated and often chaotic, the State first attempted to control river traffic with an Act of Parliament in 1514 aimed at fixing fares. A further Act in 1555 drew up the 'Rulers of all Watermen and Wherrymen working between Gravesend and Windsor'. This led to the formation of the Company of Watermen and Lightermen. Their livery hall, built in 1780, is still open at St Mary's Hill, EC4.

By 1600 it is estimated that there were 40,000 people earning a living transporting people and goods across the river. The Company ran a seven-year apprenticeship, something like the Knowledge for today's black cab drivers. Watermen were prone to disease, due to the river pollution, especially after the invention of the flush toilet, which turned the Thames effectively into an open sewer. Boatmen faced two other great risks – violent crime, normally committed at night, and attempting to 'shoot the bridge'.

The ancient London Bridge so restricted the flow of the river, due to the numerous waterwheels constructed between its nineteen piers, that the water rushed with awesome force between the central navigable arch. The difference in height was over 5ft at high tide, and it is estimated that 30 people lost their lives in the furious waters every year.

Whitehall Palace

Westminster

WITH OVER 1500 ROOMS STRETCHING ACROSS 23 acres from Northumberland Avenue to the current Houses of Parliament, this was once one of the largest royal palaces in Europe.

The home of the British monarchy from as early as 1049, its heyday was during the reign of Henry VIII. His annexing of Cardinal Wolsey's property – along with his expansion of the palace (adding tennis courts, a bowling alley, a tilting yard used for jousting and a cockpit) – cemented its place at the heart of government, a position the area has retained to this day. It was here that Henry VIII married both Anne Boleyn and Jane Seymour.

In 1622 James I had the Banqueting Hall built. It was designed by Inigo Jones, with a ceiling painted by Sir Paul Reubens. Ironically, it was outside this last major Whitehall expansion that James I's ill-starred son, Charles, was beheaded on 30 January 1649.

The Banqueting Hall was one of the few buildings to survive a fire in 1691 that destroyed much of the Palace's magnificent medieval structure, as well as many fine works of art, including Michelangelo's sculpture of Cupid and Holbein's portrait of Henry VIII. The great London diarist, John Evelyn, recorded the following day: 'Whitehall burnt! Nothing but walls and ruins left.'

Wren's Lost Churches

IT IS INCREDIBLE THAT SO MANY OF SIR
Christopher Wren's churches were destroyed, many lost
to Victorian developments:

CHURCHES DEMOLISHED:
All Hallows, Bread Street; All Hallows the Great, Lombard Street; All
Hallows, Lombard Street; St Antholin, Watling Street;
St Bartholomew, Exchange; St Benet Fink, Threadneedle Street;
St Benet, Gracechurch Street; St Christopher-le-Stocks, Threadneedle
Street; St Dionis Backchurch, Fenchurch Street;
St Matthew, Friday Street; St Michael, Bassishaw;
St Michael, Crooked Lane; St Michael, Queenhithe;
St Michael, Wood Street; St Mildred, Poultry
CHURCHES LOST FOR OTHER REASONS:
St Mary Magdalene, Fish Street (gutted by fire 1886).
CHURCHES WHERE ONLY THE TOWER REMAINS:
St Alban, Wood Street (destroyed by bombing in 1940);
St Anne's Church, Soho (demolished in 1953 after war damage)
St Dunstan in the East (destroyed by bombing in 1941)
St Mary Somerset, Thames Street (demolished in 1871)
St Olave, Old Jewry (demolished 1888–9)
CHURCHES DESTROYED BY WORLD WAR II BOMBING:
Christ Church, Newgate Street (only ruins remain);
The Cloisters, Pump Court, Middle Temple (1940–1);
St Augustine, Watling Street (1945); St Mildred, Bread Street (1941);
St Stephen, Coleman Street (1940);
St Swithin, Cannon Street, (1941)

Ackerman's 11
Adam and Eve Tea Gardens 12
Adam, Robert 36, 68
Agar Town, Kings Cross 13–14
Agar, William 13
Albert, Prince 65, 87
Aldwych 36–7
Alhambra Theatre 14–15
Alleyn, Edward 136
Alsatia 15–17
Apollo Club 46
Archer, John 74
archery 17–18, 112
Aris, Thomas 38
Astley's Circus 18, 20
Atmospheric Railway 20–1

Bach, J S 32
Bambridge, Thomas 73
Bank 105–6
Bankside 81–2, 135–6
Barbican 21–2
Barham, John 40–1
Bartholomew Fair 22–5
Baum, John 43
Baynard's Castle 25–6
Bazelgette, Sir Joseph 180
bear and bull baiting 75, 94–5,
    135–7
Bear Gardens, Clerkenwell 94–5
Bedlam Hospital 27–8, 49, 143
Belair Park 56
Belasyse, Thomas, 1st Earl of
    Fauconberg 68
Bell Tavern, Kilburn 106–7
Berkeley Square 36, 87–8
Bermondsey 102–3, 144, 155, 158
Betterton, Thomas 114
Bishopsgate 27, 29
Blackfriars 25–6, 109
Blackheath 143
Blake, William 11, 159
Blessington, Countess of 85
Blitz, the, 9, 21, 110, 124
Blondin, Charles 14, 92
Boleyn, Anne 53, 188
Bon Marché 29
Bonaparte, Napoleon 56
Booth, Charles 157
Borough 107–8, 177–8
Boswell, James 164
Boyle, Robert 100
Brandon, Richard 159
Bridewell Palace 30–1
British Museum 51, 69
Brixton 29, 55
Brummel, Beau 89
Brunner Mond chemical factory 165
Bullock, William 56
Bunhill Fields 143

Burford's Panorama 87
Burton, Decimus 40–1
Byron, Lord 65

Camden 47
Cannon Street 33, 171, 186
Carlisle House 32–3
Carlyle, Jane 88
Casanova 32
Castaing, John 105–6
Catherine the Great 35
Cato Street conspirators 38
Cave, Edward 80–1
Cecil, William 64–5
Charing Cross 33
Charles I, King 33, 159, 162, 165,
    188
Charles II, King 47, 61, 76, 114, 136
Charles V, Holy Roman Emperor 30
Charlton 98–9
Chaucer, Geoffrey 177
Chelsea 42–3, 50–2, 147–50
Chelsea Bun House, Pimlico 34–5
Chesterton, George 38
Chippendale's Workshop 35–6
Christie, John Reginald 152–4
churches, Sir Christopher Wren's 189
Cibber, Caius 27
City of London 17, 21, 52
Civil War, British 60–1, 83
Clagett, Chrispus 134
Clap, Margaret 121–2
Clare, Lord 36
Clare Market, Aldwych 36–7
Clegg, Samuel 20
Clerkenwell 38–9, 94–5, 128–9
Coldbath Fields Prison 38–9
Coleman, George 100
Coleridge, Samuel Taylor 38
Colosseum, Regent's Park 40–1
Coral, Joe 90
Cornelys, Mrs 32, 36
Cornhill fire (1748) 106
Costermonger's Language 41–2
Cosway, Richard 11
Cottington, John 'Mull Sack' 46–7
Cotton Library of Manuscripts 62
Covent Garden 35–6, 132–3
Crapper and Company Ltd 42
Cremorne Gardens 42–3
Cromwell, Oliver 46–7, 54, 68,
    74, 159
Cross, Edward 65
Crosse & Blackwell 68
Crossing Sweepers 44–5
Crystal Palace 86
Cuckold's Point 98–9

Daguerre, Jacques 47
Dance 'the Younger,' George 127

Darwin, Charles 88
d'Avenant, Sir William 113
d'Orsay, Count 85
de Berenger, Charles Random 43
de Coverley, Sir Roger 184
de Montfort, Simon 52
De Paris, Robert 135
Death Hunters 137–8
Defoe, Daniel 99, 127, 142, 143
Devereux, Robert 60–1
Devil Public House 46–7
Dickens, Charles 9, 13, 20, 73, 85,
    87, 102, 156
Dioramas 47–8
Dog and Duck Public House 48–9
Dog Finders 49–50
Don Saltero's Coffee House 50–2
Duke's Company 114
Dulwich 55–6
Durham House, The Strand 52–4

Earls Court 112–13
Edward I, King 33
Edward III, King 109
Edward IV, King 26
Edward the Confessor 179
Edward VI, King 31, 64, 172
Edwards, George 78
Eel Pie House 54–5
Effra River 55–6
Egyptian Hall 56–8
Eleanor of Castille 33
Elizabeth I, Queen 16, 17, 60, 64–5,
    74, 76, 94, 136, 162, 172, 181
Enon Chapel 58–9
Essex House 60–2
Euston Arch 62–3
Euston Station 21, 62–3
Evans, Timothy 153, 154
Evelyn, John 111, 160, 163, 188
Execution Dock 63–4
Exeter House 64–5

fairs 22–5, 29, 61, 75–7, 98–9,
    131–2, 158–9
Farr, James 147
Farringdon Market 66–7
Fauconberg House 68
Field of the Forty Footsteps 69
Fitzwalter, Matilda 25
Fleet Debtors' Prison 70, 72–3
Fleet Marriages 70–1
Fleet River 30, 73–4
Fleet Street 15, 46–7, 147, 164–5
Frost Fairs 61, 75–7

Gaiety Theatre 77–8
Gamages 79–80
Gandhi 96
Garrick, David 36, 81, 84

Gentleman's Magazine 80–1, 150
George, Chelsea 49–50
George I, King 112
George II, King 34
George III, King 18, 34, 89
German traders 171–2
Giffard, Henry 83–4
Giovanelli, Edward 91–2
Globe Theatre 81–3, 135
Goldsmith, Oliver 81, 132
Goodman's Fields Theatre 83–4
Gordon, Frederick 96
Gordon, Lord George 127–8
Gordon Riots 72, 160
Gore House 85–6
Grand Union Public House 28
Great Exhibition (1851) 86, 87
Great Fire (1666) 9, 21, 65, 72, 109, 116–17, 125–6, 160, 163, 172
Great Globe 86–7
Grey, Lady Jane 26, 53, 98
Guildhall 23, 25
Gunter's Tea Shop 87–8

Hand, Richard 34–5
Hanover Square Rooms 89–90
Hardwicke, Lord 71
Harringay Stadium 90–1
Haydon, Benjamin 57
Henry III, King 21, 52
Henry VI, King 63
Henry VIII, King 15–16, 17, 26, 27, 30–1, 53, 72, 130, 135
Highbury Barn 91–2
Highbury Tavern 92
Hillocks, James Inches 92
Hippodrome Racecourse 93–4
Hitchin, Christopher 122
Hockley-in-the-Hole 94–5
Hogarth, William 27, 31, 133, 164, 183
Holbein, Hans 30, 188
Holborn 79–80, 96, 110, 121
Holborn Restaurant 96
Hollingshead, John 78
Holy Trinity convent 97–8
Hone, William 147–8
Hook, Robert 27, 28
Horn Fair 98–9
Hornor, Thomas 40
Houndsditch 131–2
Houses of Parliament 179
Hyde Park 86, 155

Imperial War Museum 28
Islington 25, 100–1
Islington Spa 100–1, 107

Jacob's Island 102–3, 155, 158
James I, King 16, 54, 83, 109, 128–9,

172, 188
James II, King 68
Jenny's Whim 104–5
John Douglas, Maquis of Queensbury 113
John, King 25, 98–9
Johnson, Dr Samuel 48, 81
Jonathan's Coffee House 105–6
Jones, Inigo 162
Jonson, Ben 46

Katherine of Aragon 30–1, 53
Kemp, William 140
Kensington 85–6
Kenwood House 36
Kidd, Captain 64
Kilburn Wells 106–7
King's Bench Prison 107–8, 160
Kings Cross 13–14
Kings Road 42, 43
King's Wardrobe 109
Kingsway Theatre 110
Knightly, T. E. 145

Ladbroke Grove 93–4, 152–3
Lambeth 49, 183
Lange, Lord Mayor Robert 186
Langham Place 145–6
Lansdowne House 36
Lawson, Lionel 77
Le Poor, Richard 52
Leicester House 111–12
Leicester Square 14–15, 86–7, 111–12
Leno, Dan 13–14
Léotard, Jules 14, 92
Lever, Aston 112
'Liberties of the Fleet' 70–1
Lillie Bridge Grounds 112–13
Lincoln's Inn Fields Theatre 113–14
Liverpool Street Station 27, 143
London Bridge 77, 115–17, 130–1, 187
London Bridge Waterworks 116–17, 187
London Salvage Corps 117–18
London Stock Exchange 105–6
London Stone 9, 33
Lord Chamberlain's Men 81–2
Louis XIV, King of France 35
Louterbough, Philippe de 47
Lowther Arcade 118–19
Lyons Corner Houses 120

Madden, H. H. 85
Mansfield, Lord 36
Marble Arch 181–3
markets 21, 36–7, 66–7
Mary I, Queen 26, 162
Marshalsea Prison 63

Matilda, Queen 97
Mayfair 87–8
Mayhew, Henry 44, 49, 50, 67, 123, 131, 138, 144, 158, 174–6, 180, 181
Michelangelo 188
Miles, Jonathan 105
Milton, John 22
Minories, Tower Hill 97–8, 158
Molly Houses 121–2
Moorfields 27
Morice, Pieter 116
Mother Clap's, Holborn 121
Mudlarks 122–3
Muggletonianism 159
Mull Sack (John Cottington) 46–7
Munden, Sir John 51
museums 27, 28, 49, 51, 56–8, 165
Musgrove, Lord Mayor 25

Neckinger, River 155
Necropolis Railway 123–4
Negri, Domenico 87
New Gaiety Theatre 78
New River Head 54, 128–9
New Tunbridge Wells 100–1
New Westminster Theatre 18
Newgate Prison 125–8, 182, 183
Newnham-Davies, Lieutenant-Colonel 96
Newton, Sir Isaac 97–8
Nine Elms Railway Station 129–30, 185
Nonsuch House 130–1
Novello, Ivor 78

Oates, Titus 127
Odell, Thomas 83
Old Bailey 125–6, 142, 153
Old Clothes Exchange 131
Old Slaughter's Coffee House 132–3
Old Street 140
Onslow, Arthur 68
Oxford Street 32, 133–4

Palmer, Sir Thomas 64
Pantheon, Oxford Street 32, 133–4
Paris Gardens 135–7
Patterers 137–8
Peasants' Revolt 72
Peck, River 155
Peerless Pool 140
Penny Gaffs 138–9
Pepys, Samuel 23, 61, 111, 113–14, 136, 143, 160, 184
Petticoat Lane 131
Phillips, Sir Richard 149–50
Piccadilly 56–8, 120
Pillories 121, 141–2, 159, 162
Pimlico 34–5, 104

Pitt, Moses 72–3
Plague Pits 142–3
Preston, Christopher 95
prisons 27, 31, 32, 38–9, 43, 63,
    72–3, 107–8, 125–8
Proms, The 145–6
Prynne, William 142
public houses and eateries 11, 12, 28,
    46–7, 48–9, 50–2, 54–5, 87–8, 96,
    104–7, 120, 132–3, 147, 177–8
Pure Collectors 144

Queen's Hall, Langham Place 145–6

Rag Fair 131, 158–9
railways 9, 14, 20–1, 123–4, 129–30
Rainbow Coffee House 147
Raleigh, Sir Walter 54
Ramsey, Abbot of 22
Ranelagh Gardens 35, 147–50
Ratcliffe Highway 150–2
Regent's Canal 13
Regent's Park 18, 40–1
restaurants and public houses see
    public houses and restaurants
Reubens, Sir Paul 188
Rich, John and Christopher 114
Richard I, King 171
Richard II, King 107
Ridley, Archbishop 31
Rillington Place 152–4
Robert, Earl of Essex 60
Robinson, G. F. 56
Romans 9, 150, 155, 160, 161,
    178, 186
Rookeries 102–3, 156–8
Rose Theatre 135
Rosemary Lane 158–9
Royal Albert Hall 85, 146
Royal Marionette Theatre 119
Royal Panoptican of Arts and Science
    (Alhambra Theatre) 14–15, 87
Royal Toxophilite Society 18
Russell Square 69–70

Sabini, Darby 90
Sadler, Mr 100–1
Sadler's Wells Theatre 101
Salmon's Waxworks 164–5
Salter, James 50, 51–2
Samuda Brothers 20
Sawyer, Tom 13
Scott, Sir Walter 16
Second World War 21, 98, 101, 130,
    146, 186, 189
Serpentine, the 155
Seymour, Jane 135, 188
Shadwell, Thomas 16–17
Shakespeare, William 81–3
Shelbourne, Lord 36

Sheppard, Edward 84
Sheppard, Jack 127, 182
Shoreditch 140
Shorter, Lord Mayor Sir John 23
Sidney, Robert, Earl of Leicester 111
Silvertown Explosives Factory 165
slang 41–2, 138, 166–70
Slaughter, Thomas 132
Sloane, Sir Hans 50–1
slums 13–14, 37, 54, 156–8
Smith, Albert 118–19
Smith, Albert Richard 57–8
Smith, James 'Rosebery' 29
Smithfield 22, 67, 139
Smollett, Tobias 108
Soho Square 32–3, 68
Southey, Robert 69
Southwark 20, 28, 48–9, 107–8, 117,
    135, 160–1, 177–8
Soyer, Alexis 86
Speakers' Corner 183
Spencer, Charles 79–80
sports venues 90–1, 93–4, 112–13,
    140
St Bartholomew's Hospital 23
St Bethlehem's Hospital (Bedlam)
    27–8, 49
St Clements Inn Fields 36
St George's Fields 28, 107, 160–1
St Giles Rookery 156, 182
St James Park 155
St Luke's Church, Chelsea 43
St Margarets Lothbury 186
St Paul's 21, 33
St Paul's Cathedral 161–3
Stapleton, Walter 60–1
Steelyard, Cannon Street 171–2
Stow, John 21, 63, 97, 140, 171, 186
Strand, The 11, 52–4, 58–9, 60–1,
    64–5, 77–8, 118–19, 162
Street Cries 172–4
Street Traders 174–6
Swift, Jonathan 34, 74, 81

Tabard Inn 177–8
Tatler magazine 52, 164
Temple 15–17
Temple Bar 29
Thames, River 15, 42, 53, 55, 73, 75–
    7, 122–3, 155, 160, 179, 180, 186
theatres and concert halls 14–15, 18,
    32–3, 77–8, 81–4, 110, 113–14,
    133–4, 138–9, 145–6
Thistlewood, Arthur 38
Thornbury, Walter 37, 59, 62, 66, 151
Thorney Island 155, 178–9
Toshers 180–1
Tottenham Court Road 12, 120
Tower Hill 60, 97–8, 158
Tower of London 25, 60, 109

Tussard, Madame 57
Tyburn 122, 127, 155, 181–3
Tyburn, River 155, 178
Tyers, Jonathan 184–5

Vauxhall Gardens 49, 148, 149,
    183–5
Vauxhall Water Works Company
    55–6
Victoria, Queen 9, 86

Walbrook, River 155, 186
Walpole, Horace 84, 134, 148–9
Walsh, John 69
Wapping 63–4, 150–2
Waterloo Station 123–4, 130
Watermen 187
Wellington, Duke of 87
West Ham 165
Westbourne, River 155
Westminster 33, 52, 178–9, 188
Westminster Abbey 179
Westminster Bridge 187
Westminster Palace (Houses of
    Parliament) 179
Wheatley, Francis 11
White Tower (original Tower of
    London) 9
Whitechapel 83
Whitefriar's Monastery 15
Whitehall Palace 188
Whittington, Richard 125
Whyte, John 93, 94
Wilberforce, William 85
Wild, Jonathan 95, 122, 127
Wilkes, John 108, 160
William III, King 68
William the Conqueror 9
Wolsey, Cardinal 53, 188
Wood, Henry 145
Wotton, Sir Henry 82–3
Wren, Sir Christopher 161,
    163, 189
Wyatt, James 133
Wyld, James 86, 87